The blurring boundary of the organisation:

Outsourcing comes of age

Margaret Hurley

Christina Costa

Foreword by **John Rundell**

Cover art by **Jacquie Green**

Edited by **Robert Stafford**

Copyright © 2001 by Margaret Hurley and Christina Costa.

The authors assert the moral right to be identified as the authors of this work.

This edition Copyright © 2001 by KPMG Consulting (Australia).

Cover art Copyright © 2001 by Jacquie Green.

Published by: **KPMG Consulting (Australia)**

161 Collins Street, Melbourne Vic 3000

ISBN: 0 646 41573 5

Type-setting by: **Pacific Client Publishing**

Level 10, 616 St Kilda Road, Melbourne Victoria

Printed by: **Griffin Press**

Netley, South Australia

This book is copyright. Apart from any fair dealing for the purposes of private study, research, criticism or review as permitted under the Copyright Act 1968, no part may be stored or reproduced by any process without written permission.

The recommendations in this text are the result of broad-based research and are meant as guidelines. This publication has been developed to inform readers of important business trends and issues. The information contained herein should not be relied upon or used as a substitute for detailed advice or as the sole basis for formulating business decisions.

The information in this book is distributed on an "As Is" basis, without warranty. While every precaution has been taken in the preparation of the book, neither the authors nor KPMG Consulting nor the Nolan Norton Institute shall have any liability to any person or entity with respect to any loss or damage caused or alleged to be caused directly or indirectly by the instructions contained in this book.

Typeset in 10/16 Gill Sans Light

Atos
Origin

PROGRAMMED
MAINTENANCE
SERVICES
LIMITED

HANSEN
CORPORATION

hp
invent

ADP
Employer Services
Payroll & HR Solutions

AUSTRALIA
POST

T-Systems

MONASH
UNIVERSITY

ASPECT
Information Technology Solutions

KPMG Consulting Australia

KPMG Consulting Australia is a leading provider of Internet integration services. We help clients achieve sustainable competitive advantage in the new e-business economy.

In Australia our 1000 experienced professionals deliver wide-ranging services and innovative solutions to assist in the positive transformation of business. Understanding that the future is about increasing the value of clients' organisations in a fluctuating market, KPMG Consulting helps clients excel by providing industry specific solutions in the following industries: Public Sector; Financial Services; Consumer and Industrial Markets; Content and Communications; and Health, Education and Community Services.

KPMG Consulting ranks as one of the world's largest consulting operations. Globally our 17,000 employees in 157 countries ensure we have the skills and resources to serve the regional and global needs of business.

We provide the right people, processes and technology to resolve complex business issues thereby enhancing client profitability and growth opportunities.

Additional information about the firm is available at www.kpmg.com.au

Nolan Norton Institute

Since its formation in the mid 1970s, the Nolan Norton Institute (NNI) has investigated management trends, approaches, practices and solutions in areas where "the book hasn't yet been written".

As the global research arm of KPMG Consulting, NNI is the birthplace of many commonly used management frameworks and metrics, including the Balanced Business Scorecard; the Stages Theory of IT Development in Organisations; the Creative Destruction approach to Organisational Transformation; IT Benchmarking; and the hidden costs of computing.

With this publication, we have "written the book" on outsourcing.

Outsourcing today is redefining business. Organisations realise that they are not 'good at everything'. Few are now self-reliant from go to whoa – the days of vertical integration are gone.

But outsourcing approaches are maturing too. What was commonplace in the early 1990s is now no longer appropriate. The tightly written recipes of that era won't do in the age of increasing globalisation and rapid change.

The Nolan Norton Institute is once again breaking new ground with this book. It is the definitive text on outsourcing – for both buyers and service providers. It shows the way to success – focus, specialisation, co-operation, alliances, partnership, risk-sharing, and interdependence.

The Nolan Norton Institute has once again provided new, innovative know-how and skills for business.

We are pleased to commend this book to leaders in industry and government – and, together with KPMG Consulting, we encourage you to read, learn, and debate its lessons.

Contents

Foreword

Outsourcing almost invariably coincides with significant change. Change is accompanied by a wide range of phenomena, positive, negative and even neutral. In large measure because it's an easier and more dramatic story to tell, much of the press about outsourcing has highlighted mistakes or problems that may have been associated with it. As a result, outsourcing is seen by many with primarily negative connotations.

In several surveys conducted by KPMG on outsourcing in Australia, New Zealand, the United Kingdom and Europe we have found that although there were some "problems", overall, outsourcing was considered a positive strategic and operational initiative.

For over 10 years, I have sought to advise organisations on establishing outsourcing arrangements and solving problems in existing outsourcing. Over this period, the industry has evolved tremendously. The lessons learned through experience have been applied to delivering better outsourcing. This accumulated experience has much to tell us about what makes for successful outsourcing. The majority of press and research fails to address the success stories. It is time to apply some considered balance and I believe that this book does so.

We set out three years ago to find out what makes for successful outsourcing. The authors, Christina Costa and Margaret Hurley, with the support of Mark Probyn and key personnel from Monash University, have analysed nine outsourcing cases that were proposed by participating service providers. There are common themes through these cases and finally we have a text that should be essential reading for everyone – from those considering outsourcing for the first time to outsourcing veterans who want to get more out of their outsourcing relationships to service providers looking to position for the future.

The cases are from across the Asia Pacific region including Australia, New Zealand and the Hong Kong SAR.

The nine service providers (they are not just suppliers) that participated in this study include international (global) companies, government owned (in the case of Australia Post) and local specialist companies.

I was pleased to find a willingness from both the service providers and their clients to participate in this study. I was delighted with their insightful contributions.

I believe this reflects well on all organisations that participated and highlights their aim to better understand the success factors in outsourcing.

There is much activity in the outsourcing realm that goes on well beyond the large-scale, top tier service providers. This book represents a very good cross-section of the future of outsourcing, including many of the nimble and responsive "second tier" of service providers. The considerable insight that these players provide here further fuels the debate over when and whether size matters in outsourcing arrangements. Sometimes scale is exactly the right thing. And sometimes a customer is much better off with the smaller provider who "tries harder". It's key for both buyers and service providers to go into an arrangement knowing the difference.

The cases cover a range of outsourced services: IT; payroll and human resources administration; mail services; facilities maintenance; applications services; and fulfilment. The factors that lead to success are not specific to the type of service and the recommendations in the book are applicable to all parties involved in outsourcing arrangements.

I trust that this book will become a reference for successful outsourcing and confirms that outsourcing has indeed come of age.

John Rundell
Outsourcing Practice Leader, KPMG Consulting

Acknowledgements

We would like to express our thanks to those service providers and their clients who participated in the study. This program would not have been possible without their ongoing contributions and personal commitment.

Service provider	
ADP Employer Services	**Bronwyn Anderson**
Aspect Information Technology Solutions	**Graham Miller**
Atos Origin	**Lucinda Thomson** **Darryl Luttrell**
Australia Post – Mailroom Solutions	**Graham Hughes,** **Warren Hahnel,** **John Maher**
POST groceriesonline DELIVERY	**John Raphael,** **Rob Gray**
Hansen Corporation	**Mark McMullen,** **David Bevan**
Hewlett Packard	**Chris Gibbins,** **Glenn Heppell**
Programmed Maintenance Services	**Danny Shafar,** **Colin Frauenfelder**
T-Systems	**Michael Rudd,** **Jon Sturgess**

We would also like to express our thanks to the many experts who shared their experiences and opinions with us, in forums formal and informal. Thanks to the members of the outsourcing practice at KPMG Consulting for getting the program going, particularly John Rundell for sponsoring the project; and to the Nolan Norton Institute for its ongoing contributions. Particular thanks to Mark Probyn, Senior Manager at KPMG Consulting, for his extensive contribution to Chapter 3.

In addition, thanks to Dr Nicholas Beaumont, Professor Amrik Sohal and Liam Page from Monash University, for their contribution to selected cases and analysis of the survey data. Special thanks to Nigel Kelly for his support of the authors' endeavours.

Thanks to our editor, Robert Stafford, who kept us on the straight and narrow, accepting no "guff".

Chapter One

WHAT'S IT ALL ABOUT?

Outsourcing is not a new concept. Businesses have been using outsourcing since the early 1960s. It has existed in the form of application development contracts, facilities management agreements and time-sharing deals for several decades. In 1963, Ross Perot's Electronic Data Systems (EDS) was performing data processing services for Frito-Lay and Blue Cross[1]. Current outsourcing has changed significantly since these earlier arrangements. The differences relate to the operational, technical and financial sophistication of outsourcing vendors and the flexibility of their offerings. Such variants have contributed to the outsourcing business gaining popularity, as evidenced by increasing press coverage.

This research has identified that outsourcing trends have further evolved. Some of the major trends that are discussed in further detail in this chapter include: shorter-term contracts are more frequent; reputation and geographic reach of the service provider plays a key role; SLAs are living documents; and users have accepted that they need to tap into outside resources to access best practice and the best employees.

Outsourcing and contracting: does size matter?

The wholesale rejigging of companies, departments and organisations that has come to be associated with the term "outsourcing" is fast becoming a stereotype that fails to describe the norm. The prospect of outsourcing strikes fear in many organisations, suggesting an evisceration of the organisation and large-scale job losses. While the fear may or may not be justified, based on circumstances, the supposition that "outsourcing" means a complete removal and replacement of functions is increasingly an incorrect one. The concept (and reality) of outsourcing in that mode still exists and is going strong. The term, however, now stretches to include long-familiar organisational approaches, including opportunistic contracting and marginal load balancing. The classic cases of outsourcing (Kodak, Australian Federal Government, AMP Insurance, Ansett Australia, Mercantile Mutual, and the Commonwealth Bank of Australia) demonstrate the value in specialisation. But these models work under a framework that requires, in many instances, real scale in order to meet what are largely cost-cutting objectives. Those objectives have been met in a great many cases, but the opportunities to do dramatic, scale-based, cost-cutting-related outsourcing are drying up. The low-hanging fruit of economies-of-scale outsourcing arrangements has been plucked in many cases. The current story is that subtler, more flexible and more imaginative approaches to the challenges of effectively and efficiently obtaining, retaining and applying resources are required.

The low-hanging fruit of economies of scale outsourcing arrangements has been plucked; subtler, more flexible and imaginative approaches are required.

Client/server and distributed computing models are cases in point. These models demonstrate that the next step after achieving economy in volume is to reach economy in distribution and customisation. Saturation of larger markets should not mean the end of the line for products and services, if adaptability to a variety of (smaller) markets is achieved. Taken to its logical conclusion, this view suggests that a vendor should be able to adapt to serve, profitably, a market of one. ERP vendors have faced this issue in dramatic fashion. Vendors such as SAP and Baan experienced huge success, growth and profitability throughout the 1990s. Their economic model and market focus were based almost entirely on large organisations. This strategy worked so well that these vendors had effectively penetrated the market to its virtual limit. The ability of such firms to continue to grow depended on their adaptability to a wider market – they had to adapt or die. Their respective fates have turned on this very factor, with SAP surviving and pushing hard in the small-business market, and Baan's fortunes shrinking substantially.

In the outsourcing arena, this phenomenon has meant the proliferation of many new, smaller vendors. These smaller providers resemble the small-time contractor of old in many ways – but it isn't the same as it used to be. Economies of distribution and the client/server model partially describe the difference. The prevalence of technology and the assumption of access to a wide pool of expertise – all customised to the market – distinguish the current situation from the contracting of old. The requirement for all levels of service provider to have that access and reach is working to keep the marketplace dynamic. The pricing and partnerships that worked last year will not necessarily carry over into success this year.

In a successful outsourcing arrangement, it is important to understand the correct approach to apply in a given situation. There are a huge number of variables to weigh in determining the best way to manage. Size, scale, geographic locale, financial wherewithal, government obligations, corporate objectives, core capabilities, future direction – all of these play a role in devising an optimum arrangement.

Shorter contracts provide buyers with greater flexibility and an alternate way of managing risk.

The current trend in Australia is for shorter contracts with durations of about three years (with the option to extend an additional two years)[2]. Most of the outsourcing deals of the early1990s had contracts that lasted anywhere from five to 10 years. Research from the US has also found that long-term IT outsourcing contracts may be falling out of favour with many large corporations. Dissatisfied with poor performance and missed goals, major companies are scrapping old and highly generalised deals in favour of smaller, more focused agreements.[3] Shorter contracts provide buyers with greater flexibility and an alternate way of managing risk. In addition to time-flexibility, the best outsourcing agreements are fluid, with changes triggered by events and informed interaction, not by constraining clauses cast in legal stone. Long-term contracts (seven- to 10-year deals) simply can't anticipate what market conditions will be like during the life of a contract. The trend to shorter contracts brings the "old school" of outsourcing closer to the concept of contracting. In practice, the emerging models are very much a combination of contracts, alliances, partnerships, outsourcing arrangements, management imagination and innovative deal-making.

The Australian IT outsourcing market is dominated by three big players: IBM Global Services Australia (IBM GSA), EDS Australia, and Computer Sciences Corporation (CSC)[4],[5]. There are two reasons to pay attention to this fact: first, the size of the IT outsourcing market is substantial in Australia and is a bellwether for outsourced service provision in the region. Second, none of these major providers is local. There is a requirement, at the top end of the market, to have global reach and deep pockets. Size really does matter when you're a service provider – it influences whether and how you can capture a market.

In practice, the emerging models are very much a combination of contracts, alliances, partnerships, outsourcing arrangements, management imagination and innovative deal-making.

An ancillary issue related to size is the recognition factor. Large, better-known organisations (be they customers or suppliers) have a reputation and therefore an intuitive, established or earned level of trust. For entities that are unknown to each other or to the general population, the establishment of credentials becomes more important. With new and emerging business, this is more difficult. When an organisation or a service offering is well along the maturity curve, "credentialisation" is easy because a track record has been established and documentation and references can usually be called upon.

That said, the argument that outsourcing is only viable for large players is fallacious. In a rapidly-changing market, innovation is as imortant as size. In the words of a small, successful and global outsourcer, "All the good and important things that have been done have been done by small groups of people."[6] The implication here is that invention and agility are as necessary for staying power as are size and recognition. The options for large firms, then, are either to acquire or to cooperate with the smaller, more agile firms. Or lose out to them in key areas of competition.

Given that many creative sourcing arrangements resemble some sort of hybrid, or even an old-fashioned, short-term employment contract, it is often surprising that so many entities flaunt the term "outsourcing". The surprise comes not because the term may be deemed technically incorrect, but because it's so fraught with negative connotation. Virtually every government and corporate environment in the world gets a collective shiver whenever the topic arises. Dwelling on "outsourcing" versus contracting may seem like an overemphasis on semantics, but when dealing with a sensitive issue, language is very important.

Who's the boss?

The loyalty and affiliations of life-long employment are virtually gone. The dominant employer/employee paradigm of the 20th Century was characterised by long-term relationships and a pronounced identification of employees with the company for which they worked. That relationship and its underlying assumptions have changed considerably. In addition to a significant shift in the composition of the workforce (through the gradual blurring of the white collar/blue collar distinction, for example), a majority of professionals are demonstrating allegiances to entities other than their nominal employers. Professionals are loyal to their peers, to their teams and to their profession. The company is not at the top of the loyalty list[7]. This is reinforced by findings of this research study (see Chapter Five), wherein the employee base of the participating service providers was surveyed. Among participating companies, employees showed by far the strongest loyalty to the specific group of individuals with whom they work.

Professionals are loyal to their peers, to their teams and to their profession. The company is not at the top of the loyalty list.

Many factors have contributed to this phenomenon. One of them is an almost predictable tit-for-tat response to the downsizing that began in the 1980s: companies were showing diminished loyalty to employees, and employees have responded in kind. Decades of downsizing have destroyed trust in organisations and in traditional career paths. The result is an irreversible mood of diminished loyalty particularly in places like banks and the public sector.

Another, sometimes less obvious, factor is demographics: when large segments of the population (read Baby Boomers) are reaching their professional peaks, there is often insufficient room to house them all in the tiny triangles at the top of the hierarchical structures of large organisations[8]. The response of many is to leave and become a 'big fish in a small pond', diving into any environment in which they can realise their full intellectual and earning potential. Baby Boomers are having an impact on the workforce in other ways: they have reached a point in their lives where, freed of dependent children and mortgages, they no longer need to maintain a full-time commitment to the workforce.

It's not just the older generation who are aloof from corporate concerns. This freewheeling attitude to careers is most apparent in the generation that is beginning to enter positions of power – the so-called Generation X. Their dominant driving forces are a desire to control their own destiny and achieve a balance between their private and working lives. Industries, particularly legal and accounting firms, are clearly having trouble coping with these new demands. They are left wondering why young people don't want to become partners; they don't understand people who might not want to work 60-70 hours a week and, when asked to choose between a job and life, choose life.[9]

The diminishing loyalty cuts two ways: both employers and employees are demonstrating behaviours that assume a changing expectation for loyalty.

It is not uncommon for individuals to carry multiple business cards, to act in multiple professional capacities, in order to meet personal goals of intellectual challenge, professional development and income maximisation. The diminishing loyalty cuts two ways: both employers and employees are demonstrating behaviours that assume a changing expectation for loyalty. Employers, seeking maximum output, are becoming heavily performance-based in their reward systems. Employees are looking for shorter-term reward, since long-term job security is difficult to assure (from either employer or employee perspectives). Loyalty and commitment are to the profession and to performance. Outsourcing epitomises this idea, with recompense related strictly to meeting the terms of a performance agreement. In practice, an outsourcing situation is more involved than that (particularly where "face time" and on-site service provision are part of the arrangement).

It is important therefore, in managing externally sourced workforces, to understand where individual and group loyalties lie. In some instances, the employer is merely the issuer of the pay cheque – the employer's client is the one with whom a worker identifies. Whether this is advantageous for the parties involved is a matter for explicit assessment. If this is assessed incorrectly, there will be a lot of errors in attempts at incentive and reward, for example.

It's alive!

The much-dreaded service level agreement (SLA), necessary, stalwart and perhaps boring offshoot of the creative sourcing process, is (or should be) a living document. Though considerable satisfaction might be taken from the idea that the detailed process of developing an agreed set of satisfiers for a job done correctly might actually have an end point, that satisfaction is necessarily short-lived. If a SLA is worthwhile and useful, it must change over time, with circumstances. This means that when a need is changed, there isn't a cringe about how it can be incorporated into the current agreement: the process for describing, adjusting, pricing and measuring the requirements will have been established and the job simply gets done, with all attendant changes to the SLA. There is a long-standing school of thought that says that a good

SLA is one that is well planned before the contractual arrangement is entered into and that therefore undergoes virtually no subsequent change. Keep it on the shelf, admire it, laminate it – it's done.

If a service level agreement is worthwhile and useful, it must change over time, with circumstances.

That would be the case if the market and products were static, if we were dealing in an entirely "dumb" market where there is no mutual learning over the course of customer interactions. In a "smart" market, a vendor's offering changes based on interaction with the customer[10]. The view for many services is that there is far too much change in the marketplace for any agreement to stand unrevised for any substantial period of time. For services that are provided based on pre-set schedules and standardised deliverables, there is less likelihood that frequent adaptability will make sense. For services that are necessarily responsive to prevailing conditions, ones that change in nature depending on circumstance (examples include taxis, web chat, restaurants, systems development), a fluid approach to the guidelines that constitute satisfactory service provision must be established. The type of service level agreement that is appropriate will depend on several factors, including the nature of the core service and the relative maturity of the offering (placement on the life cycle curve).

Adaptability and responsiveness as regards contractual agreements can be a slippery slope. It is easy for a relationship to slip into a vortex of endless contract refinement. It is not unheard of for organisations to put so much effort into trying to anticipate every possibility that the contracting process costs more that the goods or services under consideration[11]. Adapt and grow the SLAs, but do not take it to the point of obsession.

Adaptability and responsiveness as regards contractual agreements can be a slippery slope. It is easy for a relationship to slip into a vortex of endless contract refinements.

Life cycle dictates the relationship

An understanding of life cycle maturity is essential in making informed and effective management decisions in outsourcing. A grasp of the relative positioning of both the offering and the buyer in terms of innovation life cycle is imperative. Life cycle placement determines, more than any other factor, the de facto nature of the outsourcing agreement.

Life cycle placement has little to do with the age of the organisations involved. Neither is size necessarily a factor. Large, older companies are often well served by services provided by small upstarts, and vice versa. The relationship is most influenced by the life cycle placement of the specific offering. It's not the company that's offering the service, but, rather, the maturity of the service itself.

The relationship is most influenced by the life cycle placement of the specific offering.

A classic outsourced service is payroll processing. Payroll processing is a service offering that, at its core, is at the mature end of the standard product life cycle. The type and nature of the offering are well established and known, there are expectations for pricing, and there is a lot of competition, a well-oiled infrastructure for service provision and other indicators that the service is readily available and likely quite cost-effective. The relative positioning of vendor and customer are different for such a mature offering than for a less-defined service such as Web hosting. These statements apply whether the companies offering the services are themselves young or mature – it is the service itself that has the highest correlation to the factors of greatest interest: availability of skills, quality of service, price, predictability, customisation and reliability.

Sometimes it's strategy – and sometimes it's just business

The first, breakthrough outsourcing jobs were strategic decisions. The approach to sourcing that involved, in effect, a divestiture of part of the business was a dramatic change from the traditional approaches of vertical integration and even diversification. These early outsourcing forays were significant strategic gambles that often carried a company's future in the balance. For most organisations currently considering outsourcing options, to say that the decision is one of equivalent strategic import is probably an overstatement. With mature offerings, and in cases where it's been done before by others, it is far more a tactical than a strategic decision. This doesn't make one outsourcing arrangement better or worse – it just reinforces the idea that the approach that will be most successful depends on the situation. If an organisation is treating a tactical decision like a strategic one (or the other way around), then it is likely to look for results using inappropriate timeframes and inappropriate measures. The important thing is to recognise the level (strategic or tactical) at which the organisation is dealing when a decision is being made.

If an organisation is treating a tactical decision like a strategic one, then it is likely to look for results using inappropriate measures.

The days of vertical integration are gone, and there are very few organisations that are realistically self-reliant, end to end. The total process is therefore best performed by a kind of corporate consortium, each member contributing its unique expertise. As technology advances and competitive pressures grow, it becomes increasingly unrealistic for companies to think they can be world-class at everything – and being second-rate at anything threatens competitive performance. Since everything must be done excellently, the question becomes what to do for yourself and what you should have others do for you[12].

The automotive industry illustrates how outsourcing has become a competitive imperative. First, it was total vertical integration; then the automotive industry made a practice of outsourcing the manufacture of parts and components to a myriad of suppliers. Today, automotive manufacturers have expanded the practice to include the design, manufacture and assembly of increasingly complex systems and modules, thereby shrinking the immediate supply base to a set of first-tier suppliers.

In doing so, automotive manufacturers have moved beyond vaunted just-in-time (JIT) relationships with suppliers to integrated supply and modular consortia relationships. While many firms in various industries are still struggling to implement JIT concepts within their respective supply chains, these manufacturers are championing supply-based management innovations that transcend the JIT approach and drive greater manufacturer-supplier interdependence. These partners are introducing new approaches to production as suppliers take on more of the value-added work. (Skoda's two facilities in the Czech Republic producing the Felicia and Octavia models; Volkswagen's modular consortium in Resende, Brazil; and DaimlerChrysler's Smart Car production facility in Hambach, France are representative of such evolving relationships.) As first-tier suppliers in the automotive industry are moving to modular supply, contract manufacturers in the chemical industry are taking on responsibility for the application of current good manufacturing practice, regulatory compliance and clinical testing as they build and nurture long-term relationships with their customers, the major chemical firms[13].

Historically, the automotive industry was against outsourcing and many functions were kept in-house for fear of losing control. But they have now realised that they can outsource a function and still retain control by forming a team with explicitly defined roles related to managing the outsourcing relationship. The examples above elucidate how the industry has changed to accept outsourcing as a common business tool/or practice. It is not only about control, but also about manufacturers realising that they cannot be "good at everything".

It's all about getting good people

Topping the list in virtually every survey on the reasons for outsourcing is access to skills. With loyalty changing and employment arrangements evolving, it is increasingly difficult to keep good people. While this situation is most pronounced in high-tech jobs, it is true even for low-tech jobs or for jobs where there is no shortage of qualified personnel. When there's a glut of people, there is still a job in screening, managing and retaining them. Regardless of the qualifications that a job requires— be it entry-level or highly advanced work – all organisations are interested in getting the best people available. People hold the knowledge, people hold the relationships and people do the job. Getting the best ones, getting the ones that are loyal to you (and/or loyal to your customers), keeping them motivated – these are the differentiators.

Regardless of the qualifications that a job requires, all organisations are interested in getting the best people available.

Some service industries have carried this concept to such an extreme that their attitude flies in the face of conventional wisdom. This apparent heresy is the idea that the customer does not come first. In order to provide customers with the best possible service, the customer actually ranks second on the list. Number One is the worker, the employee. If that person is happy, fulfilled, challenged, aware and adjusted, he or she will automatically see the customers' needs and do everything possible to fulfil them. This approach has been undertaken with some success in the hospitality industry, where almost every employee has some direct interaction with customers, and whose personal attitudes and satisfaction have a marked effect on customer perception.

Attracting retaining and generating top performance from their people is, in the end, the core business of any outsourced service provider. Failure in this capacity will ultimately mean failure as a business. Success will mean a multiplier of growth, credibility, innovation and profit.

Attracting retaining and generating top performance from their people is, in the end, the core business of any outsourced service provider.

References

[1]Lacity, M.C. *An Interpretive Investigation of the Information Outsourcing Phenomenon, Unpublished Doctoral Dissertation: University of Houston.*

[2]*It's Hard to Get Good Help These Days, KPMG/Nolan Norton Institute research report, 1999*

[3]*Scannell, Tim, "Putting outsourcing out to pasture? Soup-to-nuts deals at risk", Computer Reseller News, 10 May 1999.*

[4]*Howarth, B., "IT outsourcing: the next generation", Business Review Weekly, 1999, 21 (42), pp. 72-8.*

[5]*Robertson, Robert, "Size dominates the IT outsourcing market", Australian Financial Review. 28 February 2001.*

[6]*Harrison, Russell J., President and CEO of Teleias, Inc., in conversation with the author, March, 2001*

[7]*Mosley, Valerie and Margaret Hurley, "IT skill retention", Information Management and Computer Security, 1999, 7 (3).*

[8]*Foot, David, "Triangles, rectangles and workaholics: who's minding the work force?" transcript from the 4 April 1995 edition of CBC-Radio's Morningside, http://www.davidfoot.com/globe3.html*

[9]*Macken, D., "New workforce elite shifts balance of power", Australian Financial Review, 24 August 1999, pp.1, 14.*

[10]*Glazer, Rashi, "Winning in smart markets", MIT Sloan Management Review, 1999, 40, (4).*

[11]*Nolan, Richard L. and David Croson, Creative Destruction: A six-stage process for transforming the organization, Boston, Harvard Business School Press, 1995.*

[12]*Hammer, M., Beyond Reengineering, London, Harper Collins Business, 1996, p.177.*

[13]*Collins, Robert and Kimberly Bechler, "Outsourcing in the chemical and automotive industries: choice or competitive imperative?" Journal of Supply Chain Management, 1999, 35 (4), pp.4-11.*

Chapter Two
VIEW OF THE LANDSCAPE

In order to most effectively apply the lessons learned from the cases and data developed in this research program, it is helpful to review the existing body of knowledge. Many new findings are only new in their specific context: the basic precepts are often already well entrenched in management thinking. It is sometimes easy to lose sight of what we already know. When faced with new challenges, the temptation is to look for entirely new approaches. Sometimes this is warranted, and sometimes it brings one back around to some established knowledge.

For the business practices associated with outsourcing, the models and frameworks that have most relevance are those associated with understanding growth patterns and life cycles. Outsourcing has evolved from a relatively small-scale practice to a very widespread one, with attendant industry development, in the course of a decade. With a period of observable experience and a foundation in management frameworks focused on managing growth and change, we are better armed to interpret and make improvements based on what we observe now on a day-to-day basis.

The precepts of the best management thinking about growth and life cycles are reviewed and applied here to develop a subset of management frameworks for guiding today's managers through the challenges of outsourcing in the early 21st Century.

Life cycle

The life cycle curve with which we are most familiar has its roots in research done at the end of the 19th Century. The French sociologist Gabriel Tarde[14] depicted the first S-shaped curve describing propagation in research he conducted in 1890 on behaviours in societies, originating in observations of the spread, in waves, of certain crimes through society. His "laws of imitation" evolved into the models commonly used for understanding the adoption of innovations. Its basis is the idea that adoption or spread of ideas and phenomena are based on what has gone before (imitation), according to a broadly predictable pattern.

The first lesson to draw from this predecessor model is the idea that imitation is a significant driver of growth patterns. Innovation happens in the early going: growth is primarily imitation.

The S-shaped curve observed by Tarde was expanded in research by two American sociologists in 1946[15]. Their research into adoption of hybrid corn among a group of farmers produced an observation of specific categories of farmers who adopted the seed:

- innovators
- early adopters
- early majority
- late majority
- laggards

These seminal works, with their basic constructs of an S-shaped curve describing the early stages of adoption and the categorisation of adopters of innovations, have stood the tests of time and relevance. They are used today in multiple disciplines, including social sciences, medical science and commerce, among others[16],[17],[18]. In the business world in particular, the work of Everett Rogers, in his Diffusion of Innovations[19], is considered the fundamental source book in the field of innovation adoption. The major characteristics of each of the recognised groups in this model are summarised below[20]:

Innovators	Early Adopters	Early Majority	Late Majority	Laggards
• Venturesome; desire for the rash, the daring and the risky • Control of substantial financial resources to absorb possible loss from unprofitable innovation • Able to understand and apply complex technical knowledge • Able to cope with a high degree of uncertainty about an innovation	• Integrated part of the local social system • Greatest degree of opinion leadership in most systems • Serves as a role model for other members of society • Respected by peers • Successful	• Interacts frequently with peers • Seldom holds position of opinion leadership • One-third of the members of a system, early majority is the largest category • Deliberates before adopting a new idea	• One-third of the members of a system • Pressure from peers • Economic necessity • Skeptical • Cautious	• Possesses no opinion leadership • Isolates • Point of reference is in the past • Suspicious of innovations • Innovation-decision process is lengthy • Resources are limited

The precepts of this model are essential underpinnings for approaches to successful outsourcing. These basic characteristics apply to both buyers and sellers of services – the patterns of innovation and adoption are relevant to both sides of the transaction. Buyers, in order to make informed choices and set realistic expectations, must have an understanding of suppliers' positioning in terms of life cycle maturity. Is the industry in its infancy, with only a few innovators and early adopters? Is the industry mature? If so, is the particular vendor under consideration one that is operating in the mode of an early-stage or late-stage organisation?

For vendors, success depends on understanding the relative maturity of potential buyers. Is there a tolerance for risk? Is there a realistic expectation for what can be delivered? Is the profile of the potential customer a match with the offerings under consideration? This basic profiling is often overlooked, and – especially in a rapidly evolving market – can mean the difference between success and failure in both sales and delivery.

Life cycle revisited

The traditional life cycle phenomena are an essential foundation for management frameworks in the area of outsourcing. Given the pace and nature of change in the outsourcing arena, it is useful to consider more recent variants on the curves of learning and evolution implied by the life cycle curve, especially those that pay attention to emerging markets. These are the ones that can tell us the most about the least understood pieces.

Technology introductions in particular are well explained by the Stages framework of Richard Nolan. The relevance of this framework to our discussions here is that it helps us to understand whether issues that arise in the introduction of new approaches, and particularly new technology, are the result of the relative stage of the particular introduction, the relative stage of readiness of the audience for the technology or service, or the stage of the management organisation around the technology or service.

Nolan's Stages Theory focuses particularly on the introduction of information technologies in organisations. His early research on corporate expenditures on computing revealed a stage-based pattern[21] of organisational learning with similarities to the life cycle curve. Further research over the course of the burgeoning life cycle of the information technology industry resulted in relevant refinements of the original observations. First, there was a definition of the major elements, called growth processes, which undergo the staged transitions:

- applications portfolio;
- organisation;
- plans and controls; and
- user community.

These growth processes each demonstrate distinct characteristics at each of the major stages. These stage-based characteristics share indicative properties with those of Rogers, but have a further specific relevance to phenomena in the corporate world in the latter half of the 20th Century.

Specifically, the staged characteristics as described by Nolan are[22]:

Growth Process	Stage I: Initiation	Stage II: Contagion	Stage III: Control	Stage IV: Integration	Stage V: Data admin.	Stage VI: Maturity.
Applications Portfolio	Functional cost reduction	Proliferation	Upgrade	Retrofit to new technology	Organisation and integration	Systems and information flows synchronised
Organisation	Technical specialisation	User-oriented	Middle management	Utility and account teams	Data administration	Data resource management
Plans and controls	Lax	More lax	Formalised planning and control	Tailored planning and control systems	Shared data and common systems	Data resource strategic responsibility
User community	"Hands off"	Superficially enthusiastic	Arbitrarily held accountable	Accountability learning	Effectively accountable	Acceptance of joint accountability

The second significant refinement of Nolan's original theory was the recognition that the introduction of truly new major innovations result in a discontinuity of the S-shaped growth pattern: there is a jump, a leap, to a new pattern of organisational learning, analogous to the quantum leap in energy levels observed in atomic physics. Nolan defines the macro versions of these curves describing technology growth as eras[23]. The first era, the DP Era, saw the introduction of large-scale computing. The second, the IT Era, witnessed proliferation due to new, cheaper and more accessible technologies. The third, the Network Era, is characterised by the interconnection of technologies and their users on a worldwide scale.

"Organisation is but the means of which propagation (generative or imitative) is the end."

– Gabriel Tarde, 1903[24]

An underlying thesis to the Stages Theory is that fundamental organisational change must accompany effective changes precipitated by the introduction of technologies. The technologies themselves are insufficient. It is only when new (revolutionary) technologies are introduced simultaneously with substantial organisational change that the technology has any impact. Guilds and apprenticeships worked in the village and small city infrastructures and with the technologies of the time. Small family farms work very well when the primary mode of working the land is via the manual labour of man and animal. Mass industrial production works best with a hierarchical organisational construct. Each of these societal and organisational forms dominated in certain locations at specific periods in time, but evolving forces of economy and technology changed them. Technologies that enable high-efficiency farming techniques have virtually no economic advantage when applied to a small-scale operation. The confluence of new organisation around agriculture and new technology enabling farming efficiencies revolutionised society. The industrial era introduced large hierarchical organisations, something with which most of us are familiar, but which is a fairly recent phenomenon.

The requirement for massive change in organisational forms is depicted in Nolan's work as "organisational discontinuity"[25] .

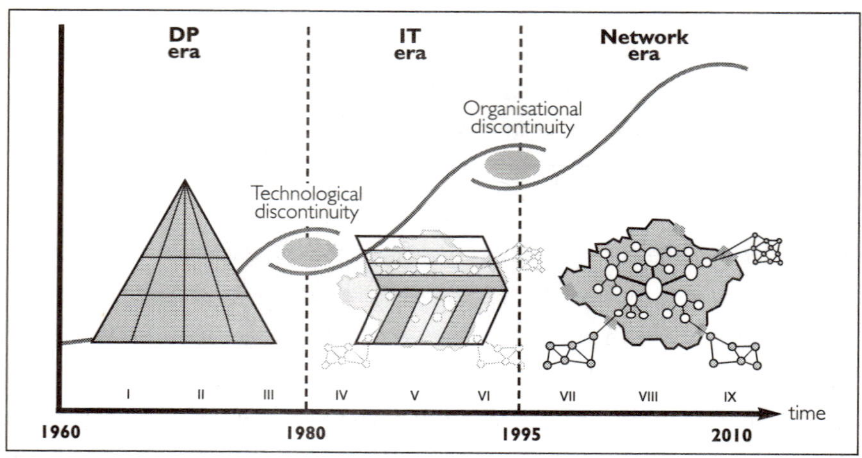

Nolan's Stages Theory

As changes in technology necessitate fundamental changes in organisation, we will see new forms of organisation become the standard. The organisational forms that are being precipitated by the phenomenon of outsourcing are the beginning of this transition. At a time when it is increasingly difficult for existing organisations to cope with the influx of innovations and economic forces, alternate forms of structure have necessarily evolved. Entities that were spread too thin to compete effectively have taken on alliances and contracts for cooperative action that are enabled by outsourced service provision.

One of the most common points of reference among the entrepreneurs at the heart of the New Economy is the Tornado framework postulated by Geoffrey Moore and the Chasm Group.[26] This framework builds on the core life cycle and organisational learning frameworks, with specific adaptations for the information economy. The Chasm Group's key framework describes an organisational, technical and economic "chasm" that must be crossed in the transition from innovation and early adoption to more mainstream and widespread acceptance. This framework has a great deal of resonance with organisations competing in an Internet-influenced economy: crossing the chasm represents the predictions that must be made about a rapidly-changing and profoundly unpredictable future, with specific profiles and strategies (the Tornado and the Bowling Alley) awaiting those who successfully make the leap[27] .

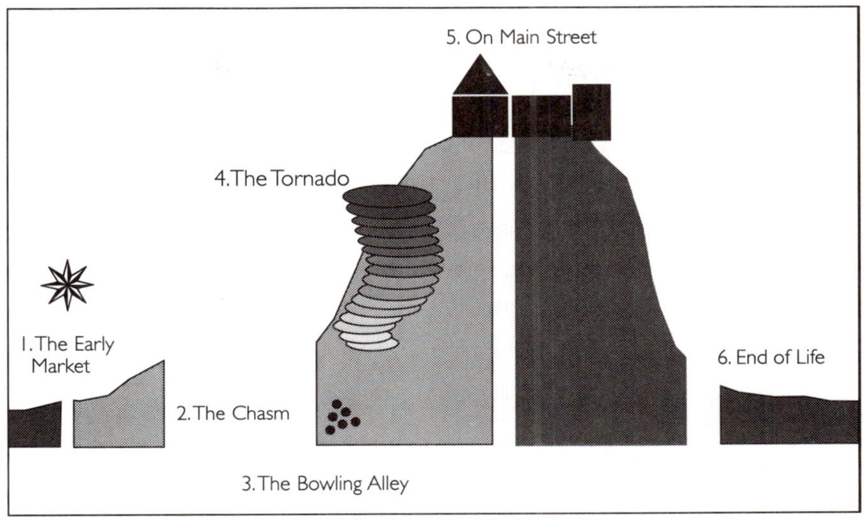

The Chasm Group's core model: crossing the chasm

This model is of particular relevance among New Economy companies due to its specific attention to discontinuous innovations: the early-stage patterns and strategy profiles are those of product and service introductions of a radically different profile than what exists in the marketplace.

The idea of discontinuous innovation has parallels in Nolan's discontinuities: they both recognise that hockey-stick-style growth patterns are closely affiliated not with straightforward improvement, but with outright innovation.

In the late 1980s, the very idea of outsourcing was a huge discontinuous innovation. As the concept was adopted, grew and gained acceptance, there developed smaller innovations around the delivery of outsourced services. Much of successful outsourcing in the early 2000s has resulted from innovation around the processes related to service delivery. These administrative innovations have been responsible for much of the later-stage growth and development of outsourcing.

Administrative innovation is defined as "involving significant changes in the routines used by an organisation to deal with its tasks of internal arrangements and external alignment"[28]. Diffusion has been suggested as a mechanism whereby an idea, such as outsourcing, spreads among organisations. There are two main competing theories of diffusion: internal and external mechanisms. The internal component is one where "the rate of increase in the number of adoptions depends on the extent in which the members of the community have already adopted the innovation"[29]. That is, companies make outsourcing decisions based on other organisations that have already outsourced. Conversely, external factors are relevant when the diffusion is driven only by information from a communication source external to the social system. That is, organisations that could potentially adopt outsourcing do so due to the efforts made by vendors, consulting firms or trade periodicals.

The Eastman Kodak decision is regarded as a turning point in outsourcing's history. Adoption was considered, in Loh and Venkatraman's[30] study, before and after Eastman Kodak's decision to outsource. The main findings of this study were that adoption of outsourcing is motivated more by internal forces and imitative behaviour than by external influence among user organisations. This is an extremely important message for vendors of outsourcing. Intimate customer knowledge is far more important in designing, selling and delivering a successful offering than is any conventional marketing and sales campaign.

In the context of diffusion and imitation, Lacity and Hirschheim[31] have described this type of imitative behaviour as the 'bandwagon effect'. They argue that outsourcing is often a response to the hype and publicity surrounding the subject, which leads senior management to ask, "Why don't we outsource?" Lacity and Willcocks'[32] study reinforces this finding, demonstrating that 38% of respondents cited 'jump on the bandwagon' as a reason for outsourcing. The Loh and Venkatraman study provides stronger explanations for the 'Kodak Effect' by using administrative innovation theory.

As outsourcing, as an innovation, has reached a more advanced diffusion stage, the applicability of administrative innovation theory in today's outsourcing environment is open to question. Intangible aspects of human behaviour are usually ignored in most of the literature that examines the impetus for outsourcing. The case studies outlined in Chapter Four begin to answer the question of why people outsource and what factors they may or may not be imitating as they pursue it. Given what we know about the practice of outsourcing in the region and the areas that have reached high levels of adoption, we can describe the region's major outsourcing offerings against our key frameworks[33].

Early-stage offerings, those that are still undergoing innovations and may not yet have crossed the chasm, include Application Service Providers (ASP) and Ergonomics services (building more productive work environments). Fulfilment and Business Service Providers are very much in the potential high-growth stages. Certain well developed areas have incorporated administrative innovation to precipitate a discontinuity and result in a spin-off of other offerings: IT and accounting are the prime examples. Stalwarts such as building and facilities maintenance are mature and well understood and are focused primarily on constant incremental improvements and innovations.

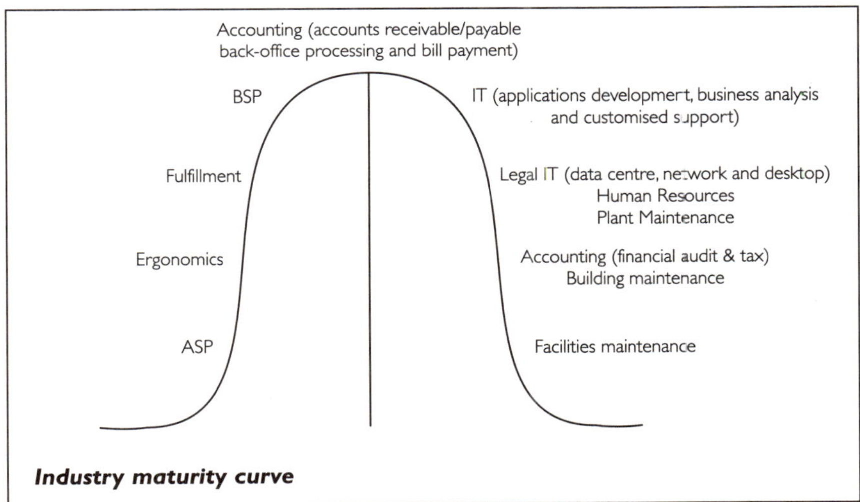

Industry maturity curve

Partnership and cultural fit

Given that the range of outsourced offerings runs the gamut from fledgling to very mature, it is clear from what the life cycle frameworks tell us that each of these offerings will have different commercial characteristics. The fundamental component of an outsourcing arrangement is the contract. The specifics of the contract are discussed in more detail in Chapter Three. The general nature of the contract, given life cycle placement, is of interest here. The nature and terms of an agreement can vary tremendously depending on whether the parties to the agreement view each other as allies, partners, suppliers, general merchants or some other descriptor. The contract's nature will also depend on the maturity of offerings, and whether or not there is competition in the market. The implementation timeframe for the service (and therefore whether there are significant barriers to entry for competitors once a supplier is in place with a customer) and the sharing of risk are also influencing factors.

Due in large measure to the newness of the concept of strategic sourcing partnerships, outsourcing arrangements that are considered "partnership arrangements" are deemed to be, by definition, somehow "better". Of course, it is always preferable to be in an arrangement where one is treated as an equal, as the term "partner" is formally defined. But the ability to employ the concept realistically depends very much on the relative position of the two (or more) parties. Sometimes a plain old supplier/buyer relationship is the best arrangement – it forces competition on merits, not history.

The nature of the relationship is influenced by another view of the life cycle: what are the respective viewpoints of the potential partners? If there is not clear mutual understanding of objectives at a high level – why are we in this arrangement? – there is room for wide misinterpretation of specific details.

For example, incentives and rewards may seem straightforward, developed with a specific end in mind. Organisations should collectively understand any behaviour that they are trying to encourage. An excellent example of an organisation that didn't get it right is a North American bank that set out to bring in more mortgage business. In order to achieve the increase, they focused on the salespeople, rewarding them monetarily for the volume of new mortgages they brought in the door. The bank got a great deal more mortgage business, but it also ended up with tremendous load of mortgages that went into default.

In this case, the interpretation of the desired action on the part of the bank's direction-setting team was considerably different than that of the sales team. Both were working toward a commonly stated – but differently interpreted – goal. The direction-setting team provided in good faith a set of monetary incentives for a set of actions. The sales team acted in good faith to bring about the encouraged result: more mortgages. The interpretation of "more" business was not the same between the groups. It was lack of a common view, of a common mindset, that caused the true goal of the organisation to be missed.

The lesson here for outsourcing arrangements is that for that elusive state of true partnership to be achieved, there must be a true mutual view of what constitutes success.

Another common area for missteps in outsourcing arrangements is in cultural alignment between the organisations concerned. Cultural fit is too often viewed as a single "thing", but it is multi-faceted. At the very least, a cultural view should differentiate between social and corporate cultures; values; mores; the difference between individual and company matches; and the reliance on history, trust and relationships.

In the end, it is previous history that makes the difference. There is some requirement for both parties to engage in dialogue, to "suck it and see". In the establishment of trust – the key element in both partnerships and cultural compatibility – a previous history with the potential business partner is by far the greatest influence[34,35]. This point is further punctuated by the finding that most organisations with successful electronic commerce relationships rate formal agreements as very low in importance, relying instead on dealing with known entities in an established manner[36].

Many previous studies have emphasised the importance of culture in the success of the relationship. The cases documented in this research, however, show a somewhat different pattern. In fact, some of the companies described each other's fundamental cultures as very different, yet this has not affected the success of the relationship. This forces us to explore whether it is culture we are describing or rather the working relationship or stage of maturity.

For many, the answer lies in alignment. Are both buyer and vendor viewing their positions in roughly the same way? Do they see themselves as doing a straight outsourcing bid, or are they more inclined toward an early-stage, share-the-risk, new-organisational form? The work of KPMG's worldwide outsourcing practices has resulted in a useful depiction of the continuum between these basic forms[37].

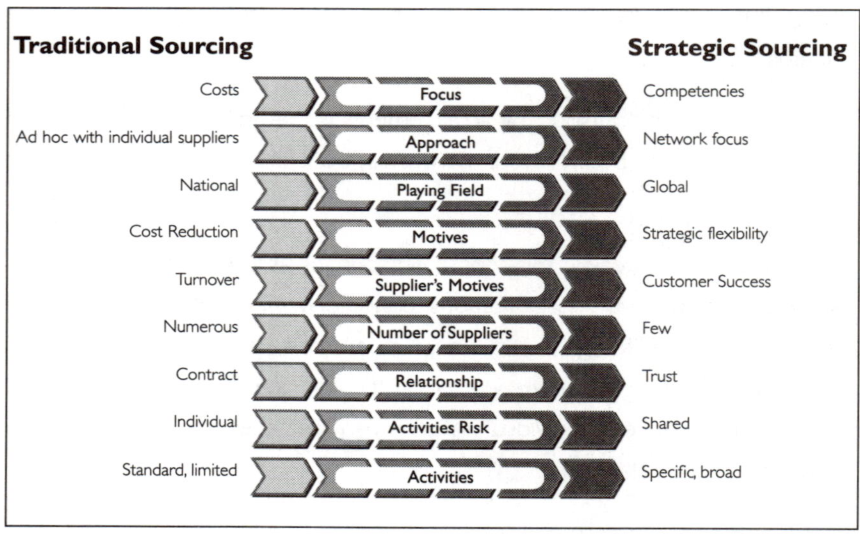

Strategy vs. tactics

Given the emphasis on early-stage tactics and the dramatic innovations of many well known outsourcing initiatives, it has become something like conventional wisdom that any outsourcing arrangement is going to be a strategic-level decision. But that is not always the case.

The CIO of a multinational oil corporation described outsourcing as "a method of rebuilding the focus of the organisation so that you focus on what is important to the organisation, and not what is important to the traditional IT world"[38]. This argument is frequently cited in the literature. It is thought that organisations should focus on their core competences and activities, while contracting out peripheral activities that the market can perform more cost-effectively and/or which distract an organisation from its core activities. This view is supplemented by the long-standing desire on the part of many organisations to use outsourcing as a means of accessing skills[39]. Hence outsourcing is viewed as a strategic decision that may cause far-reaching repercussions through the entire organisation.

The decision is not as simple as the strategic-versus-commodity approach would suggest. Lacity, Willcocks and Feeny's (1995) study[40] identified the following important findings. First, although a particular function may be viewed as a commodity, it may be too critical to hand over to an outsider. Similarly, an activity that is seen as business-critical or strategic does not necessarily have to have all of its elements kept in-house. For example, the fact that a function is strategic may not necessarily mean that the IT systems supporting that function are also strategic. Hence IT being viewed as strategic does not necessarily translate into the belief that the organisation ought to retain ownership and control of the production process for IT. The highly publicised Kodak outsourcing contract is an example of an organisation outsourcing for strategic advantage.

This argument may also be linked to resource-based theories. For example, firms may lack the talent and skills to develop potential core differentiating applications. Under such circumstances, researchers have suggested it is advisable to outsource core functions.[41]

The study conducted by Willcocks, et al[42] offers an acceptable framework that provides a starting point for further examination. The main findings are that it is best to outsource a non-core activity – that is, activities that do not act as strategic differentiators. The researchers also argue for organisations to undertake targeted, not total, outsourcing as a way of minimising risk. There is perhaps a degree of researcher bias in this, since UK outsourcing, in comparison to US outsourcing, tends to promote selective outsourcing over total outsourcing.

The authors also developed a set of frameworks "to clarify options and aid managers in deciding which function to contract out and which to retain in-house"[43]. The researchers proposed the following framework to help organisations determine which activities to outsource.

Contribution of Activity to Business Operations

Critical	Best Source	Insource
Useful	Outsource	Eliminate or Migrate
	Commodity	Differentiator

Other researchers support the argument of viewing the selection of functions to outsource based on their contribution to the business by stating: "if the function is not seen as 'core' to adding value but only is seen as a cost-reduction mechanism or a support service, then it should be considered as a prime candidate for outsourcing"[44]. They go on to say that since management is responsible for maximising shareholder value, outsourcing non-core functions has become an important business tool.

Organisational options

The organisational discontinuities surrounding the growth of outsourcing are resulting in the emergence of structures and specific roles expressly related to outsourcing. Some of these are discussed in more detail in Chapter Five. Two of them merit mention here, as harbingers of the broad changes and patterns associated with the maturing of outsourcing.

In successfully crossing the chasm to a viable and growing entity, outsourced service offerings rely increasingly on the establishment of a Steward, someone who takes specific responsibility for balancing the requirements and expectations of all parties to an outsourcing arrangement. Stewardship[45] is the

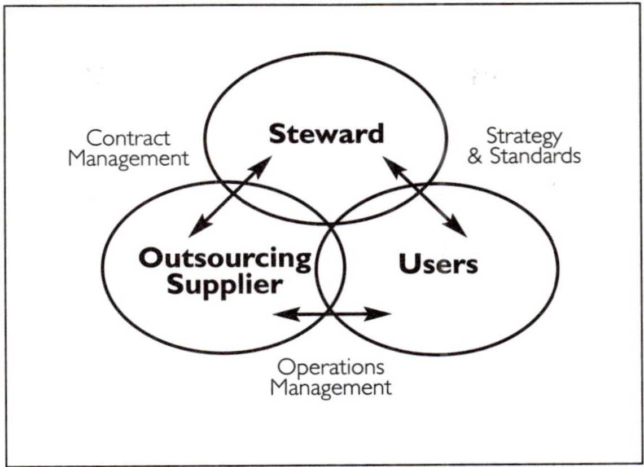

relationship management between clients and suppliers. For a client, Stewardship is the proactive management of the supplier as an "informed buyer". In this role, as displayed below:

- The User is responsible for exploiting the service to generate value
- The Supplier is responsible for delivering the service demanded in accordance with the framework of contracts, standarcs etc.
- The Steward is responsible for creating and maintaining the frameworks within which services are delivered and exploited – that is, contracts, standards, strategies, budgets etc.
- The successful Stewardship arrangement requires the establishment of a responsible committee in the buyer's organisation. The Management Committee enables the Steward to represent multi-business units with disparate business objectives. The committee members' main function is to ensure the alignment cf resources for maximum business benefit. They would endorse or approve all policy, planning and many management decisions.

Having made a successful progression, some organisations are recognising the maturity of a portfolio of outsourcing agreements and are supporting the establishment of an executive-level position for managing this asset. The Chief

Resource Officer[46] has responsibility for the full range of resources in and outside an organisation as they relate to effectively managing the skill and related resource needs of an organisation.

The view from here

A review of the research and literature on outsourcing in the region provides several key lessons for those trying to manage outsourcing. Underlying all of them is a need to view the elements of outsourcing against its life cycle positioning. This fundamental is crucial to making the right decisions.

Imitation and innovation

The first notion to understand is whether growth and reaction are the results of innovation (and therefore in very early stages) or of imitation (and therefore closer to high growth). The actions taken should be very different based on this differentiation. Innovations will appeal to early adopters and should be sold to that specific market. Imitation can follow any of a number of patterns and those should be understood to the extent possible. This will affect the level of readiness of both vendors and buyers in the marketplace.

Discontinuity and leaps of faith

There are transitions – between an innovation and widespread adoption, and between maturity and a possible rebirth – that are predictable in the product life cycle. Whether the transitions are successfully achieved depends on whether they are accurately anticipated by those most affected. Successful transitions rely on dramatic leaps, whether they are termed discontinuities or chasms, and those that fail to attempt them will not cross the void. The outsourcing industry is undergoing so many dramatic changes that there must be a constant view of an organisation's capability for taking such leaps at any point in time.

New organisational forms

The changes and growth under discussion go hand in hand with organisational change, of which outsourcing is a huge component. These organisational changes are inevitable in the transition of economies from industrial to information age constructs. The specific forms that will become standard are open for debate, but the trade-offs between buyer/supplier relationships and partnership development are being tried and tested every day. Along with these changes comes the development of organisational positions that have never before been needed, including ones that only exist for managing outsourcing relationships. Understanding life cycle placement is as relevant now as it was in the days of Tarde, if not more so. Life cycle placement dictates virtually all of the important management elements of outsourcing: strategic (or tactical) placement; supplier readiness; buyer readiness; relationship form; and likelihood of success. In a rapidly changing and difficult environment, a reliable and well tested basis, with new tweaks for changes in the environment, can't help but serve managers well.

References

[14]*Tarde, Gabriel, Les Lois de l'Imitation, 3rd Ed., Paris, 1890.*

[15]*Ryan, B and Gross, N.C., "The diffusion of hybrid seed corn in two Iowa communities" Rural Sociology, 1943, 8, pp.15-24.*

[16]*Clarke, Roger, "A Primer in Diffusion of Innovations Theory" http://www.anu.edu.au/people/Roger.Clarke/SOS/InnDiff.html*

[17]*"Diffusion of Innovations", NASA HQ Library, http://www.hq.nasa.gov/office/hqlibrary/ppm/ppm39.htm*

[18]*Calvo, Arlene and Kristi Rahrig, "Diffusion of Innovations", http://www.med.usf.edu/kmbrown/Diffusion_of_Innovations_Overview.htm*

[19]*Rogers, Everett, Diffusion of Innovations, 4th Ed., New York, The Free Press, 1995.*

[20]*Hornor, Marianne S., "Diffusion of Innovation Theory", http://uts.cc.utexas.edu/~mshech/paper1.html, (?1998)*

[21]*Gibson, Cyrus and Richard L. Nolan, "Managing the four stages of EDP growth", Harvard Business Review, January-February 1974.*

[22]*Nolan, Richard L., "Managing the crisis in data processing", Harvard Business Review, March-April 1979.*

[23]*Nolan and Croson, op cit., p. 7*

[24]*Marsden, Paul, "Forefathers of memetics: Gabriel Tarde and the laws of imitation", Journal of Memetics - Evolutionary Models of Information Transmission, 4. http://www.cpm.mmu.ac.uk/jom-emit/2000/vol4/marsden_p.html.*

[25]*van der Zee, Han and Paul van Wijngaarden, Strategic Sourcing and Partnerships, Addison Wesley, Amsterdam, 1999, p. 37.*

[26]*Moore, Geoffrey A., Crossing the Chasm: Marketing and Selling Technology Products to Mainstream Customers, HarperCollins, New York, 1991.*

[27]Moore, Geoffrey A., *Inside the Tornado: Marketing Strategies From Silicon Valley's Cutting Edge*, HarperCollins, New York, 1995.

[28]Loh, L. and N. Venkatraman, "Diffusion of information technology outsourcing: influence sources and the Kodak Effect", 1992a, Information Systems Research, 3, p. 337.

[29]ibid., p. 340.

[30]ibid.

[31]Lacity, M.C. and Hirschheim, R., Information Systems Outsourcing – Myths, Metaphors and Realities, John Wiley & Sons, New York, 1993.

[32]Lacity, M.C. and Willcocks, L.P., "An empirical investigation of information technology sourcing practices: Lessons from experience", MIS Quarterly, 1998, 22 (3), pp. 363-408.

[33]Battiston, John, Margaret Hurley and Christina Costa, "Market Overview", presentation to the working group Successful Outsourcing in Australasia, Melbourne, July 2000.

[34]eCommerce Trust Study, Cheskin Research and Studio Archetype/Sapient, January, 1999.

[35]Ratnasingham, Pauline, "Implicit trust levels in EDI security", Journal of Internet Security, Ottawa, February, 1999.

[36]Electronic Commerce: The future is here, Nolan Norton Institute, Melbourne, 1999.

[37]van der Zee and van Wijngaarden, op.cit. p. 54.

[38]Lacity and Willcocks, op.cit., p. 1.

[39]Hurley, Margaret and Folker Schaumann, "The IT outsourcing decision", Information Management and Computer Security, 1997, 5, (4), pp. 126-132.

[40]Lacity, Willcocks, and Feeny, "The value of selective IT outsourcing", Sloan Management Review, 1996, 37, pp. 13-25.

[41]Saunders, C., M. Gebelt and Q. Hu, Achieving success in information systems outsourcing, California Management Review, 1997, 39 (2), pp. 63-80.

[42]Willcocks, L., M. Lacity and G. Fitzgerald, Information technology outsourcing in Europe and the USA: assessment issues, International Journal of Information Management, 1995, 15, pp. 333-351.

[43]Lacity, Willcocks and Feeny, op.cit., p.13.

[44]Skinner, J. and B. Bond, "The outsourcing decision: opting for value", Australian Accountant, 1997, 67 (10), p. 42.

[45]Lowrey, Ross, "'Owning' IT: The Stewardship Role", NNI: Opinion, 1 (5), 1996.

[46]Casale, Frank, "The Rise of the 'Chief Resource Officer' (CRO)J28

, The Outsourcing Institute, http://www.outsourcing.com/buyersite/articles/risecro/main.htm (?2000)

Chapter Three

HOW TO DO IT

This chapter is intended as a primer on the basics of outsourcing. The headlines highlight the full set of basics in the subject area for those well versed in the topic, while the text is intended to provide an easily comprehensible grounding for those to whom outsourcing is a relatively new phenomenon. The chapter covers the following areas: making the decision; outsourcing models; strategies for scanning the marketplace for an appropriate service provider; general principles; and common issues regarding the design of the contract and the management of the relationship.

Making the decision

Companies are motivated by different strategies in pursuing an outsourcing arrangement. Some of these reasons include: access to skills; focus on core business; improved service quality; increased flexibility in resourcing; access to technology; managing costs; and making costs predictable. Since in-depth research has been conducted in this area, our intention here is to explain the thinking behind each strategy. The reasons stated are not mutually exclusive: instead, it is more common for a combination of these reasons to influence the decision-making process.

Access skills

Much of the impetus for outsourcing has come from areas in which the availability of skills is limited and/or the technical expertise required is very high. This is particularly the case in the IT sector where skill scarcity is already quite real. In some cases, outsourcing to an external service provider may be the only practical way to access the skills necessary to deliver services properly.

Organisations may be experiencing a shortage of highly skilled and experienced personnel brought about by retirements, resignations, caps on recruitment or an inability to recruit into the industry. Remaining employees may not always have the specialised skills or training to keep pace with the rapidly evolving technology.

In general, organisations will insource those skills necessary to support core functions and use outsourcing to access highly specialised skills that they find difficult to recruit and retain. Organisations also benefit from having their staff work with the outsourcing service provider's specialists. Those staff who are managing the contract need to maintain the currency of their knowledge in order to ensure the representation of the organisation's interests in the provision of the services.

Focus on core business

Organisations should focus on their core competencies so that they can perform their missions more efficiently and effectively.

Under outsourcing, management's role shifts from primarily managing resources and technology to managing relationships and contracts, and satisfying the needs of customers. Management, however, retains the accountability for the quality and cost of service delivery.

When an organisation concentrates on carrying out its core functions, it can use its financial, human and management resources more effectively and efficiently. Outsourcing some functions provides organisations with the flexibility to redirect resources to activities critical to their missions.

Improve service quality

Outsourcing can be an effective tool to improve customer service. Service providers may have more flexible, innovative and effective ways of delivering services and ensuring the services reach the people they are meant for. Examples of this might include offering longer service hours or flexible hours built around client use patterns, and access to services via technology.

In an era of increasing specialisation and rapid advances in technology, many organisations find that the quality of service provided in-house is not keeping pace with best practice. Aging infrastructure, poorly maintained equipment, inappropriately skilled staff or outdated work practices are deficiencies that outsourcing can address to improve service quality.

Increase flexibility in resourcing

Maintaining the level of equipment and staff necessary to cover peak loads can leave an organisation with under-used resources during low periods. Conversely, an organisation may find it difficult to maintain resources at a level sufficient to meet demand at peak periods, leading to poorer customer service. Outsourcing functions subject to peaks and troughs in usage can provide an organisation with the flexibility to respond rapidly to changing demands.

When an organisation is contemplating providing new services, outsourcing can ease the process of building the skills and resources required to respond to these new initiatives.

Access technology

Organisations also look to outsourcing as a solution to the need to keep up with the accelerating changes in technology.

Outsourcing service providers often have more funds or expertise to acquire and maintain new computing / telecommunications resources than many organisations. Outsourcing service providers are also seen to be able to implement the new technology better and more quickly because their core business forces them to focus on continuous technology refreshment. Reinvestment is crucial to survival and maintaining competitiveness, particularly when considering the fast-paced changes in the business world. Organisations are much slower about adopting and reinvesting in technology improvements.

Manage costs

Outsourcing can reduce both fixed and recurrent costs. Budget realities have a key impact on deciding which functions to perform in-house and which to outsource. In some instances, such as accessing superior services in IT systems, applications and software development, the costs may be similar or higher. In such cases the decision to outsource is driven by the business need for the superior service.

Make costs predictable

Another important benefit of outsourcing is the ability to foretell costs. The uncertainty caused by compounding rapid business change with technological change could lead to cost overruns and unpredictable cash flows. A fixed-price contract simplifies budget planning and cost management for organisations.

Earlier qualitative research[47] found that some companies value the *predictability* of costs an outsourcing contract offers more than cost savings. Not incurring an increase in costs can be equated to cost savings. This is because companies may otherwise have incurred cost increases when they take into account staff pay rises, staff bonuses and other factors. By outsourcing, the cost commitment is fixed, so contracting firms have effectively taken out insurance against unpredictable costs.

The research highlighted users' satisfaction with having a fixed contract whereby costs will not increase. Predictability of costs proved to be more valuable than cost savings. This is supported by a comment by a client organisation: "Through outsourcing we sought to gain/leverage economies of scale and provide improved service levels *at a predictable cost*. Consequently, actual costs, on paper, tend to look higher with outsourcing. However, outsourced costs are predictable, and if contracts are well managed, unplanned events can be mitigated or responded to within the scope of the engagement. Therefore, if unplanned events are considered, outsource costs are actually less than non-outsourced costs".[48]

Outsourcing models

As outsourcing has matured, a range of models has evolved into a clearly distinguishable set of outsourcing strategies. These range from a total outsourcing approach, to selective sourcing, to consortium arrangements, to insourcing, to establishing a joint venture. The appropriateness of a particular outsourcing model will depend on an individual organisation's requirements. The most commonly adopted model is selective outsourcing. This does not necessarily mean that selective sourcing is the most appropriate model to use; it simply means that the appropriateness of one model over another relates to an organisation's objectives and the risk management context. It is more significant to consider the impact and associated risks each approach has on the rapidly changing environment in which it operates.

The following section describes the various outsourcing models and provides an overview of their relative strengths and weaknesses.

Total Outsourcing

What is it?

This model involves totally outsourcing a function (generally 80% or more of a function) to a single service provider. This model receives the most attention due to perceived associated risk and the potential for large revenues for vendors.

Why would you use this model?

Reasons for deploying this model are varied. The most frequently cited benefit relates to the single point of accountability arising from dealing with one service provider. It is anticipated that the adoption of this model allows the service provider to create greater economies of scale, which increases the service provider's profitability, thus maintaining interest in the relationship. This model has the potential to minimise contracting costs and processes.

Caveat

Some of the early, highly publicised outsourcing deals adopted this model and received extensive criticism for doing so. The most commonly cited criticism linked to using this model is the feeling of being "trapped" in a relationship that may not evolve with the changes in the external environment. Practitioners and academics alike tend to regard this model as unsafe and as an inappropriate solution. Their apprehensions arise from several key factors, including: the supposed inability for a single service provider to provide the best-of-breed services across all technologies in all geographies; lack of price competition for vendor's services; potential to lose leverage through the monopoly relationship; risk of complacency by the service provider; and decrease in options/choices.

Selective outsourcing

What is it?

As the name implies, this model involves establishing a separate outsourcing contract for selected functions with services providers that are recognised as best of breed for the relevant functions under consideration. This model is the most common because it recognises that vendors have different core competencies and may not be able to do everything skilfully. It is hoped that as a result of using a vendor whose core competency is the function being outsourced, the overall quality of service will be improved. In addition, intense competition among vendors tends to produce more competitive prices.

Why would you use this model?

This model is most appropriate when a choice of best-of-breed offerings is desired. Those that are experienced in managing service providers can keep them at peak performance. This model also tends to be most appealing to clients that like the feeling of maintaining control and flexibility – provided they know how to handle it. Other benefits include: promotion of competition and prevention of complacency, thereby improving quality and performance; invoking keener pricing; and increasing flexibility in relationships.

Caveat

This model increases the complexity involved in managing multiple vendor contracts and relationships and can be problematic for those organisations not experienced in handling vendors. Its success depends on a dedicated resource managing the various relationships. This model requires greater sophistication from the client in terms of tracing accountability to relevant service providers. A true weakness inherent in this model is the likelihood of not attracting the interest of reputable service providers, as the slice of the work may be too small. Worse still, there is the related danger of attracting a service provider and running the risk that the size of the work or revenue generated may not keep the service provider interested, thus re-directing the provider's focus and best people to higher-value customers.

Consortia outsourcing

What is it?

There are two versions of what is considered best-of-breed consortia. The first involves one service provider that takes on the role of prime contractor, selecting subcontractors to fulfil service requirements. In the second version the client organisation appoints both a prime contractor and the subcontractors to work with the prime. This model is popular, since it appears to offer the benefits of choice and supposedly easier management.

Why would you use this model?

This model tends to increase flexibility and options through the provision of choices of services, service providers and best of breed methods, procedures and systems. It seeks to achieve keener prices through competition, which in turn prevents complacency. It also offers the potential to lower the cost of administration of contracted services.

Caveat

A weakness of this model is the risk that the prime contractor may not be competent at managing and providing incentives for subcontractors. Moreover, individual vendors may not be as familiar with the business needs or impacts across the enterprise as the prime supplier. The use of several contractors means no one service provider is accountable, leading subcontracted service providers to argue over ownership of problems, resulting in delays in the problem resolution process.

Insourcing

What is it?

This model represents the establishment of a separate internal business unit. In effect, it creates a pseudo-commercial entity with low risk.

Why would you use this model?

This approach ensures the best understanding of continuity of business needs. It provides an opportunity to create industry-specific competencies with the option of eventually spinning off the business unit to realise value.

Caveat

Some problems with this model are linked to human resources and staff attrition – that is, workforce retention remains an issue. This model also exhibits some finance-related issues. First, it is difficult to prove ROI for the internal operation. Second, it is difficult to control total cost of operation without forced contractual arrangement with individual business units.

Joint venture

What is it?

A service company is built with and shared with a market service provider. Outsourcing joint ventures are mostly oriented to serve the "client" partner. This model requires both parties to share common objectives and have clarity about each other's roles and responsibilities. Moreover, both parties need to contribute to the JV's development and marketing to ensure its success.

Why would you use this model?

This model allows for the acquisition of specialist skills without going through the outsourcing transition process, thus ensuring continuity of service during the deal and transition phase. This model also allows the client to retain a certain degree of control over the joint venture's resources, organisation and strategy.

The new service company can generate possible profits by performing work for external organisations in addition to supporting the internal operations of the owning companies.

Caveat

Joint ventures are the merging of components of two separate organisations to create a new organisation. The two original organisations will likely have different cultures and methods of operation, making the merger difficult. There is the potential for the new organisation to spend a lot of its time dealing with two separate internal camps, and losing focus on its reason for existing, which is to produce goods or services for the external marketplace.

Unless the economics of the joint venture make it self-sustaining through the provision of services back to both its parent organisations, it will depend upon selling its services to external clients. The marketing and sale of services may not fall within the skill domain of existing staff of the joint venture, who have been used to being an internal services centre. Careful consideration must be made as to how the joint venture will successfully market to external clients.

Shared services

What is it?

Shared Services is an arrangement whereby an organisation consolidates its internal operations of common functions into one division, or Shared Service Centre. The Shared Service Centre then supplies services to the entire organisation. A Shared Service Centre can be likened to an internal service provider.

Why would you use this model?

Organisations that have dispersed, duplicate departments may benefit from consolidating the functions into a Shared Service Centre. It can offer a number of advantages including economies of scale, greater career opportunities for internal staff in a larger, more focused department, and greater predictability of service for internal customers.

Caveat

Small to medium-sized organisations are unlikely to have sufficient operational scale to achieve any gains from creating a Shared Service Centre. Large organisations may have sufficient scale, but their culture and method of operations are such that a centralised function providing services to the entire organisation may go against a philosophy of discretely operating business units.

Creating a Shared Service Centre means the organisation needs to devote management effort to realising the gains. Simply merging separate departments into one 'super' department achieves little, and may be counterproductive if processes and procedures are not modified to optimise the operations of the new Shared Service Centre.

Finding the service provider

Organisations adopt a diverse mixture of approaches in selecting a service provider. The overriding consideration must be whether the supplier's services align with the organisation's own goals and requirements in seeking to outsource some of its activities.

Standard desiderata

In assessing the prospective service provider, the organisation considering outsourcing may have several goals:

Specialist assistance: The service provider's core competence is the outsourced service, so the buying organisation should obtain greater specialist input than it is able to develop in-house.

Economies of scale: The service provider is performing a similar function for other organisations, so it can deliver services more cheaply than the prospective buyer.

Access to technology: The service provider has greater opportunity to be at the forefront of developments in its area of core competence.

Access to new skills: The service provider will have a broader set of skills to support a variety of clients.

Cost: Through a tough commercial attitude as well as economies of scale, the service provider should be able to offer cost benefits.

Shared risk: Service providers are much better equipped to handle many risks, such as volume-related risks.

Free management time: Management can better concentrate on the organisation's core business.

A common apprehension regarding outsourcing relates to the dichotomy of client and vendor objectives; the client generally seeks either to save money or to achieve value for money while the vendor survives by making money. Bearing this in mind, the organisation should ask itself how and where the service provider is taking its profit. The organisation should understand the service provider's economics. A function should only be outsourced if the service provider's degree of efficiency covers the saving required to achieve the sale to the organisation, as well as the service provider's marketing and other expenses, and provides it with a margin.

Other selection criteria

The organisation should anticipate the service provider's cash flow requirements and consider issues such as price escalation, obsolescence and the service provider's financial strength, investment and profit. There is no point in attempting to set a fee and payment stream that will place undue financial burden on the service provider. The result of this may be that the service provider attempts to contain costs by reducing the level or quality of service. The fee and payment stream should be equitable to both parties.

The organisation should understand the service provider's mission. Is it to control the client?

Emphasis on cost reduction may inhibit innovation. A low-cost service provider – for instance, providing the outsource maintenance of mainframe legacy systems – may be competitive on price precisely because it is exploiting economies of scale without the need to be innovative or remain abreast of development in the market.

All organisations should competitively benchmark the function prior to outsourcing. Otherwise they run the risk that inherent inefficiencies will be built into the service level sought from the provider, which is to their own competitive detriment.

The promised cost benefits from outsourcing must be properly projected over the term of the contract. Some contracts are little more than over-priced leasing arrangements. The organisation's desire to preserve flexibility may mean that any cost-savings are lost in separately priced additions and variations.

The times are changing

Predicting the pace of change in the market and in an organisation's own business beyond a three-year horizon is difficult. This has implications for the optimum length of an outsourcing contract, the risk premium the service provider will demand and the way prices should be modified over the contract's life.

What is considered common currency today may be outdated processes or technology tomorrow. The organisation should seek to keep abreast of changing environments and make cost/benefit decisions on taking up new technology or processes as they become available.

The Internet revolution has highlighted the need for organisations to be able to move with the times. The speed of change in the ways organisations and people do business with the Internet has been phenomenal, fundamentally changing the way business is conducted.

No one can say with certainty what tomorrow's revolution will be. Today, more than ever, flexibility and capability to change are essential for continual business prosperity. Services provided by service providers under an outsource arrangement are no different. In fact, the need to allow the services to be changed or modified as new technology becomes available is even more important than ever. Outsource contracts are typically for a minimum fixed period. If technology advances significantly during this period, an organisation that is locked into a non-flexible contract may be disadvantaged in relation to one that has a flexible contract, or no contract at all.

Designing the contract

The contract is the basis of how the organisation and the service provider will work together. The working relationship of the two parties is ideally one of cooperation, trust and good faith. The contract will provide the framework for that working relationship, as well as dealing with the unpalatable if any aspects of the relationship don't work properly for either party.

The organisation should remember that a good contract is one that clearly sets out the obligations of both parties and, at the same time, allows both parties to work effectively. It should not be in the organisation's interest to structure a contract that is overly onerous for the service provider, either in preventing the service provider from effectively delivering the services or in putting its long-term viability at risk by meeting all the terms and conditions of the contract. In an ideal world the contract should be a *win/win* outcome. The contract should not be a *win/lose*, or, even worse, a *lose/lose* outcome, because in the long run the organisation will likely be a loser under either of these latter two arrangements.

Can't ignore legal aspects

Partnering is defined as the cooperation between two parties needed to achieve mutual business objectives. It is based on participants improving each other's skills and information to enhance overall competitiveness and performance. Partnering is distinct from the notion of a partnership in that partnering deals with the working relationship between the two parties and a partnership exists when the profit motive is shared. Partnering is not a formal contractual relationship; hence, it is not a substitute for an outsourcing contract.

It is common for outsourcing agreements to incorporate the notion of 'partnering'. However, without a contract, many legal implications of relying on a partnering arrangement remain inherent because the concept of partnering is non-specific and legally ambiguous. It is not unusual for the parties themselves to be unsure about what they intend to achieve through a partnering arrangement. In broad terms, the goal seems to be "*a spirit of cooperation that falls outside the contractual framework*".

An outsourcing arrangement has to be built on an outsourcing contract. The best outsourcing relationships develop as ones of trust and mutual benefit, but outsourcing as a rule only works if built upon detailed and effective contracts.

The foundation of a successful relationship is a well designed contract, with well defined SLAs. The SLAs specify service levels that are measurable and quantifiable. In essence, they establish the baseline for the relationship of the parties. An effective SLA requires a clear and comprehensive description of the required services and required performance levels.[49] The contract and SLAs provide the basis for successful, regular service delivery. This, in turn, becomes the platform for the trust and mutual regard that are essential in building a partnering paradigm.

Don't forget flexibility

Some outsourcing literature (for example, Earl[50]) argues that outsourcing reduces flexibility because long-term static outsourcing contracts bind a company in a relationship with the vendor that is difficult to break. The arrangements researched had, on average, contracts with a three-to-five-year duration. All contracts had renegotiation options that accommodated changing needs. Flexibility itself has many dimensions. Increased flexibility may be the ability to easily handle an increased volume of transactions, change administrative arrangements, replicate the operation in an extra location, modify software (for example, to handle the GST[51]) or run on upgraded hardware.

From the client's point of view, a long-term contract for IT services cannot be written in an ironclad manner. The importance of flexibility is that business objectives, clients' requirements, business processes and especially information technology are constantly changing and a flexible contract should allow for such changes. Hence, the interviewees prefer a flexible contract that accommodates such changes. More research is needed to determine the effect of outsourcing on flexibility (whether it be within the contract or in reference to particular functions).

"Outsourcing does not take place in a static environment. The nature of the technologies, external competitive situations, and so on are all in a state of evolution"[52]. Flexibility as a success factor has also been stressed by academics Lacity, Willcocks and Feeny[53].

The contract must be designed to provide maximum flexibility in line with required service and price. Litigation under a contract in an outsourcing arrangement is certainly not in the organisation's interest. The organisation has entered into an arrangement in which it totally depends on the service provider delivering a key service. The impact of this service being withdrawn by the service provider is likely to be severe, if not catastrophic, for the organisation.

Like a constitution, the contract has to be forward-looking without trying to foresee and legislate for every conceivable circumstance. If it does, it will be an unworkable contract. The contract should be sufficiently flexible to accommodate the organisation's changing needs and to keep pace with market innovation.

The contract should not attempt to be prescriptive about how the service provider should carry out its duties and obligations. If it is, it may inhibit the service provider from providing innovation and emerging better practices. If the service provider is discouraged from being proactive, the organisation will be responsible for investigating and keeping abreast of opportunities for improvement.

Instead, the contract should be prescriptive about the services to be delivered (the outputs). That is, the contract should be output based (services), not input based (method of delivery).

Key considerations in outsourcing contracts

A good outsourcing contract should cover several key considerations. The exact definition of the clauses will be case-specific, but in general the following should apply.

Who owns the intellectual property?

It is crucial that the contract clearly identifies who retains ownership of any intellectual property in question. It is not uncommon in an outsourcing arrangement for either party to contribute intellectual property at the start of the arrangement. Typically this property would remain the property of the original party.

A more contentious issue may be if intellectual property has been developed during the course of the arrangement. The contract should identify the means by which ownership can be identified.

Dispute resolution

The contract should clearly identify the dispute resolution process to be followed by either party. Termination of the contract should be an absolute last course of action, because the implications, particularly for the client organisation, are significant. Termination, if not planned for, can potentially place the ongoing operations of the organisation at risk.

An example of a dispute resolution process to be followed by both parties may be:

> Disputes other than non-payment of invoices are to be raised with the Contract Manager.
>
> Any unresolved disputes are to be raised at a regularly held management committee meeting. The management committee, which includes representatives from the organisation and the service provider, will resolve the dispute.

Any remaining disputes will go to mediation. Both parties agree to attend mediation, and will (or will not) be bound by the mediator's decision.

In the event of unresolved mediation disputes, the dispute can go to court, or the contract can be terminated.

Who owns the data?

The contract should clearly specify that the organisation retains ownership of all its data in the event of termination of the contract. This will also be important during reversion. The supplier must be required to return all client data in a useable form, as part of its reversion services.

Reversion services

Details of the length of reversion period, and the requirements of both parties during reversion, should be specified. Reversion periods will typically be for a period "up to x months, at the client's option".

Right to audit

The client pays for a defined level of service, and typically the service provider will provide the means to measure the actual level of service provided. The client will pay for the service on this basis, so the client must be able to audit the service provider's records to ascertain their accuracy.

An audit may take a number of forms. The client may request a copy of transaction records to verify reported data. Users may be contacted to verify user satisfaction of services provided, and at the same time a reasonableness check can be done on the level of services being reported by the service provider.

Audits are typically limited in scope to verifying performance against service levels. As such, they would not involve financial audits or operational audits outside the scope of services.

The frequency of audits is a mutually agreed issue. It may be appropriate, for instance, to conduct an audit after the initial six months of operations, and annually thereafter. An agreed notice period will be issued to the service provider, and agreed audit procedures will be followed.

Technology refreshment

In outsourcing arrangements in which a technology function is outsourced, it is often very desirable for the client to require technology refreshment clauses in the contract. If the contract is for three to five years, it is reasonable to expect that IT technology will progress significantly during the course of the contract. It is in the client's interest to ensure that the organisation is kept, at the very least, abreast of new technology, and given the options to take up new technology as it becomes available.

Services and service levels

The contract should include services and service levels to be provided. This is the basis of the arrangement entered into. It is common to include services and service levels as an attachment to the contract.

Assignment and novation

The contract should specify the process by which the service provider can assign or novate parts of the contract to third parties. The client should have the right to refuse to accept assignment or novation if reasonable grounds exist. For example, if the service provider were to attempt to assign part of the contract to either a competitor of the client, or a third party that the client chooses not to conduct business with, then the client should have the right to disallow that assignment.

Privacy

The contract should ensure that the service provider maintains adequate privacy and protection of client data. The service provider does not have the right to use client data for any purpose other than the provision of agreed services. The service provider must ensure, to the best of its abilities, that client data is protected from both intentional and unintentional distribution to third parties. This should include the provision of adequate security mechanisms, such as firewalls and secure environments.

Liquidated damages

The contract should specify the nature and level of damages payable by either party in the event of a breach of the contract. It is unlikely that either the service provider or client will accept terms that specify consequential damages, but in the event of material breaches, the damages should be commensurate with the nature of the damage incurred.

Penalties and bonuses

The contract should specify if any penalties or bonuses to the service provider are to apply. If penalties for non-performance of agreed service levels -- or bonuses for exceeding agreed service levels -- are to apply, the formula for determining the amount should be specified.

The merits of including bonuses in the contract are debatable. At one extreme, the inclusion of bonuses may modify behaviour in a positive way. Conversely, the client organisation may feel that the other side of the argument is that "you landed the contract, you're getting paid, what more do you need to motivate you to perform/fulfil expectations?" A bonus system may not be appropriate for all outsourcing arrangements. For example, a goal of answering all calls in 30 seconds or less suggests no bonuses, whereas a goal of answering calls ASAP may be compatible with a bonus proportional to reductions in response time. Alternatively, theories such as Williamson's Transaction Cost Theory[54] argue that bonuses may lead to negative behaviour by the vendors. This argument is illuminated by, specifically, the construct 'Threat of Opportunism' whereby costs may increase if the vendor behaves opportunistically.This construct suggests that human nature is assumed to take on negative characteristics, whereby people will take advantage of other parties with whom they are transacting business, knowing and understanding their self-interesting behaviour. This negative view of human behaviour imposes limitations of the theory's applicability to the emerging shift towards partnering between vendors and clients.

It is conventional for outsourcing arrangements not to include bonuses. Some companies were concerned that the inclusion of bonuses could result in the service provider focussing its efforts on bonuses rather than other areas. Such concerns may be minimised by implementing a bonus system that encourages desired behaviour. It is common for clients to conclude, in hindsight, that bonuses may be applicable in cases where some savings can be demonstrated. A particular client, in this research group, felt that the service provider was not as proactive as he would like and questioned whether the inclusion of bonuses would help.

All contracts in the cases examined had penalty clauses. The contract should be about 'conditioning' behaviour rather than 'triggering penalties'. This type of behaviour is evident in cases in which the client could have invoked penalty clauses but chose not to. The common message among the cases was that instead of invoking penalties, clients would prefer to consider why the contractual arrangement did not work (i.e., why the supplier was unable to meet the SLA) and how they can make it work. Exceptions, of course, were made in cases where damages arose.

The inclusion of formal bonuses, such as gains sharing, may become more appropriate with the maturity of the market and the relationship. It may be worth considering at the renewal point of the contract. Bonuses may create win-win situations and assist in establishing partnering relationships. Although bonuses were not explicitly stated in the contract, there is evidence of implicit bonuses, where companies chose not to impose penalties for non-performance. This indicates a shift towards a partnering relationship and the implicit existence of performance credits.

Duration of the contract

The duration should be adequate to ensure favourable terms, but not so long as to lock the customer into contracts that may become non-competitive over time due to such things as obsolete technology, prices being driven down by advanced manufacturing techniques, changed business requirements or new competitors in the market.

Other issues

The table below lists other points that should be considered when setting up the contract:

– What is the process for extending the term of the contract?
– What is the effect on the contract of a material change in the system specifications?
– What assets are to be sold to the supplier?
– What third-party contracts are to be assigned to the supplier?
– What client contracts are to be novated to the supplier?
– What personnel are to transfer to the supplier, and on what terms?
– Is a lower level of service applicable during the transition period?
– What are the parties' migration obligations?
– What is the duration of the initial term for the services?
– On what basis can this initial term be renewed?
– Have the system specifications been agreed in relation to the provision of the services?
– Has the price for the assets been agreed?
– Has the manner of payment been agreed?
– Is the supplier to provide a financial undertaking?
– Is the supplier to provide a performance undertaking?
– Is the supplier required to take out any form of insurance?
– What is the governing law of the contract?

Managing the relationship

This section summarises the tasks that must be undertaken once the contract is signed, and operations begin. Managing the ongoing relationship is the most important part of the outsource cycle. If this is done fairly and efficiently, the promises of the pre-contract negotiations have every chance of being realised. If this task is not carried out diligently, or the organisation attempts to manage it in a manner that was not anticipated pre-contract, it is highly unlikely that the contract will succeed.

Transition and handover

Although much of the contract negotiation will have been completed by this stage, often the contract is still subject to a number of criteria being fulfilled. These may include the confirmation of transition plans, confirmation of financial arrangements, payment of securities or bonds or other contract conditions.

An implementation plan, strategy and team should be established at this stage. This phase also covers the transition to the selected service provider. Formal handover of service delivery may take some time to phase in beyond contract signature and implementation. This would be the case particularly when the service is to be provided over an extensive geographical area, has a high degree of complexity or requires a substantial amount of intellectual exchange between the outsourcing department and the service provider. Timelines, responsibilities and deadlines for the implementation and transition should be established at this stage.

The skills and authority of the staff managing the outsourcing contract are important considerations when establishing the team. These internal staff will need to understand the contractual arrangements and have sufficient authority to ensure that the rest of the organisation complies with the contract. They will also need to manage the relationship with the service provider at an executive level. This is paramount to the success of the arrangement.

Human resources issues will take priority at this stage because the manner in which issues such as redundancies and staff transitions are handled can affect the morale of the entire organisation. Staff should be assisted through this difficult time as much as is possible.

The following guideline of considerations should be included in a handover plan:

- New organisational structure and timings for its implementation
- Definition of responsibilities
- Change management strategy
- Staff job descriptions, employment contracts, secondments, training, redeployment and recruitment (if necessary)
- Management of assets – a disposal or transfer strategy
- Expiry, termination and assignment plans (where necessary) for any existing third-party contracts to ensure that the outsourcing organisation does not pay for duplicated services
- Establishment of service delivery monitoring mechanisms, billing and payment processes (these must be communicated to the parties responsible as they arise)
- Preparing notification of handover and implementing approval processes
- Senior management should allow significant time for monitoring implementation progress. An independent review of the handover should be conducted, especially when the organisation is contemplating outsourcing other functions.

Service delivery monitoring, audit and relationship management

The most important aspect of the management of the contract is the finalisation of the service delivery measures. Coupled with this is the finalisation of billing procedures. It is incumbent on the service providers to provide clear, accurate invoices to allow the client to authorise them. The client must also have procedures in place to be able to process these invoices in a timely manner.

Contract performance should be monitored and evaluated throughout the life of the contract. This data will be vital when the outsourcing organisation reassesses its needs to determine whether to renew the contract or to go out to the market again.

Please note also that the organisational requirements may change throughout the life of the contract. This will also have considerable influence on whether the contract is renewed or put back out to tender.

Regular review meetings will need to be conducted at a senior level. This may be on a half yearly or quarterly basis, depending on when the reporting is due. Reviews of this nature tend to include:

- Reviewing the strategy and plans;
- Assessing actual performance against service levels and against the results of the final cost/benefit analysis;
- Using actual performance data to conduct benchmark reviews against other similar arrangements;
- Conducting quality assurance reviews; and
- Sponsoring negotiations for any contract variations.

In addition, an operational-level team will need to monitor the contract more closely. The frequency and agenda of their review meetings will change through the life of the contract. They may meet several times a week during the transition and initial operational stage (whereas afterwards they may meet weekly or fortnightly to address issues as they arise), look for improvement opportunities and identify any additional or unnecessary requirements.

If the service is not delivered in accordance with the service levels, this may be managed by attempting to resolve any issues directly with the service provider. This may involve setting up a team comprised of service provider staff and organisation staff.

As it will take a considerable amount of time and expense to effect any disengagement from the service provider, the effect of any actions on the relationship between the parties must be carefully considered.

If measures are put into place for the non-delivery scenario prior to contract finalisation, these should be managed in accordance with the documented process, which may specify withholding of incentives or imposition of penalties. If non-delivery recurs, the parties may need to consider engaging legal advisors. Initially, a conciliatory, mediated approach to solving the problems is the best strategy.

As a last resort, the parties may need to consider disengaging from the relationship prior to the natural end of the contract.

Contract administration

The contract administration function is responsible for documenting any contract variations and reissuing the altered contract to relevant stakeholders.

The contract administration function should be part of the operational-level team. It should also be facilitated/managed by the contract managers.

Please note, however, that some flexibility in the contracting process will be required because, as discussed above, this contract will be closer to partnership than a procurement contract. In consequence, all variations should be structured and drafted with this in mind.

Partnering

As suppliers understand their clients' businesses, so they are becoming a part of them. As they take on more of a client organisation's internal functions, suppliers become more critical to the organisation's success. Some relationships, involving mutual benefit and risk, can become true partnerships.

At one extreme, the most ambitious outsourcing contracts are nothing short of joint ventures in which the outsourcing organisation may take a stake in the supplier and the supplier uses the contract to develop services that can be marketed to third parties for the mutual benefit of organisation and supplier.

Suppliers are turning to strategic partnering as a way to add value and differentiate themselves. Originally, outsourcing provided suppliers with a return through economies of scale. Now that organisations identify their own benchmarked efficiencies before outsourcing, suppliers have responded by offering a partnership.

Some functions are too integral to an organisation's business to be outsourced. Some are spread across too many activities. Suppliers have come to know and understand their client's business. They seek process outsourcing opportunities that cut across organisational functions, and in that way make themselves more integral to the client and better positioned to offer strategic partnering.

Today's outsourcing contracts define existing services. When partnering is sought, the contract and the relationship management focus on acquiring and harnessing capabilities. Obtaining new value for capability from a contract demands openness of information, mutual regard for each other's capabilities, and a commitment to invest in the relationship and opportunities. A framework for sharing the benefits must also be obtained. Achieving and sustaining this is the challenge for future business management.

Summary

In this chapter we have highlighted the essential elements to be considered when entering into an outsourcing contract. We reiterated the typical reasons for outsourcing. Answering the question *why do you want to consider outsourcing?* is a crucial first step to being able to outsource successfully. The wrong reasons can often lead to the wrong results.

We discussed various outsourcing models and their strengths and weaknesses. No one solution is right for everyone, and an understanding of models that have been successfully adopted in the past provides the reader with options that will help ensure a positive outcome for his or her organisation.

We discussed the importance of finding the right service provider for your organisation. As demonstrated, this is not necessarily the cheapest, or the one that offers the widest variety of service. Considerations of cultural fit are important when entering into a contract that places great reliance on a third party for the continued provision of vital services to the organisation.

The essential elements of a sound contract were highlighted. Contract negotiations should be carefully conducted to ensure that required outcomes are not hindered by the contract. Focusing on the highlights indicated above will ensure that essential aspects of outsourced arrangements are not overlooked.

Finally, we briefly discussed managing the relationship. This is an ongoing task that must be diligently undertaken to ensure that all the promises of the pre-contract negotiations are fully realised for the organisation.

References

[47]*Costa, C. The Value and Incidence of IT Outsourcing in Australia, unpublished Bachelors Dissertation, Monash University.*

[48]*ibid.*

[49]*Wildish, N., "Outsourcing IT – safeguarding your legal interests", Purchasing and Supply Management, 1993, December, pp. 30-33.*

[50]*Earl, M., "The risks of IT outsourcing", Sloan Management Review, 1996, 37, pp. 26-32.*

[51]*Note that it may be easier and cheaper for a contractor running the same or similar software for several clients to modify software than for clients to do it individually.*

[52]*McFarlan, F.W. and R.L. Nolan, "How to manage an IT outsourcing alliance", Sloan Management Review, 1995, 36, pp. 9-22.*

[53]*Lacity, Willcocks and Feeny, op.cit*

[54]*Williamson, O., Markets and Hierarchies: Analysis and Antitrust Implications, The Free Press, New York, 1975.*

Chapter Four

WHAT MAKES US DO IT?

There are many reasons for outsourcing: timing, circumstance, geography, nature of service and industry all have an influence. The overwhelming message from nearly every study on the subject (and from virtually every interview and workshop that we've done for this study) is that the absolute centre of any successful arrangement is a strong mutual understanding of the objectives by both the customer and the service provider. With that in mind, we now review several of the most common reasons for entering into an alternative sourcing arrangement. Most of these will be supported or illustrated by a case chosen from the companies participating in the study.

Focus on the core business

Core competency leads inevitably to core business. While not always the top reason for choosing to service part of the business externally, the ability to focus on the core business is the most common – it makes the list most often. An ability to focus on the core business moves higher up the priority list the more mature the service offering. When a service is readily available in the market at a very competitive price and consistent, predictable quality – that is, when it is mature – there is a much greater likelihood that the service will be outsourced so that businesses do not have to expend resources on developing and maintaining the particular expertise in-house. Even the smallest businesses will contract out for services such as bookkeeping or cleaning. These are mature, necessary services (virtually no business can operate without them) that take significant attention and resource away from the core business.

Another permutation of the maturity-as-impetus idea is exemplified by the cases in which the internal service offering is practically post-mature – i.e., it's a laggard sort of situation. Much of the outsourcing of the servicing of Y2K problems falls into this category. The skills required to perform the service were at the very end of the product life cycle. Most companies saw a bleak picture when considering the option of nurturing in-house a set of skills that, while necessary in the short term, would be obsolete in fairly short order. This would either require lay-offs or extensive retraining, no matter how the internal sourcing was done.

The same idea applies in one of our cases – **Aspect.** The client has a legacy system with a planned replacement date. While a replacement system is under development, the old system must continue to operate reliably since it's mission-critical to the organisation. (This is an instance of simultaneously outsourcing core and non-core activity with the same action.) The function being outsourced is the day-to-day maintenance of the legacy application. The outsourced service of maintaining the still-operating old system is critical to the successful running of the business, but the day-to-day maintenance of that system is not a core function. Even Microsoft outsources the day-to-day maintenance of the PCs in its offices.

It may be argued that the displacement of payroll-related resources is primarily a question of where the activity happens, not a case of allowing resources to redirect their activities to something that is central to the business – for how many businesses is payroll a core function? But that's too simplistic. Of course, it's crucial for any business to get payroll out on time. For organisations with huge numbers of employees in a wide variety of locations and at a variety of levels of training and responsibility, and with relatively high turnover, functions related to monitoring employee patterns are essential. The strategic management of this information can make a huge difference to large retailers and franchise operations, for example. An ability to ofload the "grunt" work associated with this information – that is, its assembly and dissemination, but also controlling it and using it to improve management – represents a true realignment of resources for better focus on the core business. The case of **ADP Employer Services** illustrates this.

Case 1: Aspect Information Technology Solutions

http://www.aspect.com.au

The following case is taken from an interview with Aspect's account services manager, and another with the Chief Executive from the client organisation. The case covers the outsourcing responsibility for legacy software.

The client

In 1995 and 1996, an Australian firm that managed superannuation for a few large governmental clients, but wanted to diversify its customer base, decided to replace its entire computer infrastructure with new commercial software over several years and to outsource the maintenance of some of its legacy computer systems. Outsourcing the maintenance of the legacy systems was an appropriate solution. Maintenance, especially of old systems, can be an uninteresting task for competent computer professionals. As well, the decision to purchase replacement systems, rather than fully develop them in-house, recognised that software development was a "non-core" activity. The client continues to maintain a strong IT department that works closely with service providers and vendors.

The client's business comprises outsourced services (the management of superannuation funds) and the client well understood the nature of the outsourcing business: the client already outsourced some of its own functions such as printing and distribution of mail-outs, audit and IT help desk. "We live and die by how much we cost to run the place and what we can charge, so we've got a reasonably good understanding of those things." Some of these functions have been outsourced for a long time and the client believes that the important lesson is to develop a satisfactory relationship between the outsourcing vendor and client.

The vendor

The vendor's core business is software development and maintenance. The vendor has been providing information and technology solutions since 1974. The Aspect Group is currently the largest privately owned Australian systems integration and software development company, with computer-related revenue in excess of $A250 million per annum, more than 1,200 employees worldwide and over 6,500 customers in 68 countries.

Aspect partners with several Australian government departments and many Australian businesses. It has recently completed successful large-scale e-business projects such as the Australian Taxation Office's Public Key Infrastructure (PKI) project, the largest in the world, and the Victorian Government's *maxi* project. The *maxi* solution allows the delivery of government services and bill payments online, 24 hours a day, every day of the year.

Aspect seeks clients that share the same entrepreneurial and operational philosophy and that are willing, as partners, to venture into new terrain to investigate new means of achieving business advantage. This is especially important if the client believes that outsourcing is the best way for technology to be exploited for improved service delivery to its clients. It "...has created long-term partnerships with its customers based on trust and achievement. Some of these alliances have endured since the mid-1970s and it is not uncommon for [the vendor] to celebrate tenth business anniversaries with its customers." Aspect considers commitment to the success of the partnership to be paramount: the client to its business drivers, Aspect to the provision of appropriate technology and both to sharing the risk.

Selection

Expressions of Interest (EOI) were sought from six vendors, of which three were short-listed. The client was most concerned with "cultural fit" – that is, finding a good working relationship with an outsourcer – but considered the following factors important: the management style of the organisation; its experience with similar clients; and local experience. The client was less concerned with the technicalities and mechanics of the arrangement. The client had previous experience with outsourcing and was less concerned with the process than an organisation new to outsourcing might have been. "Our selection process was biased heavily towards making sure that we ended up with an organisation that was a good cultural fit for us rather than spending a lot of time on details, definitions within the clauses of a contract and so on."

In retrospect, it would have been better to have paid more attention to contractual details. A prerequisite imposed by the client was that the service provider had to employ the client's displaced IT employees.

A panel of three people undertook the selection process. Two members were client employees and the third was an independent. This person was neither an employee of the client organisation nor an external consultant, but rather took the role of a trusted and impartial judge. The way in which the short-listed companies behaved and operated during the selection process was influential. The successful applicant's managing director appeared in person: he was well briefed and able to answer questions immediately. A large corporation gave a standardised ("canned") presentation but was evidently unwilling to adapt to the client's particular concerns. A third applicant studied the brief but telephoned three days later, opined that the fit was poor and withdrew. This decisive action was admired: "They didn't muck us about."

The relationship

A relationship between two business entities can range from strictly arm's length to close and continuing cooperation. Unfortunately, Australian law does not recognise cooperation between entities. The cooperation necessary to a successful outsourcing operation, especially the outsourcing of a core function, has no legal basis in Australia.

Both parties considered that the arrangement was between equals. At the time, the contract was the largest that the vendor had ever entered into. The vendor was anxious to secure a project of this size and scale. Despite this, the client felt "comfortable that we were both going to get married and learn together" and noted that: "Just because the relationship is considered a supplier/buyer relationship doesn't necessarily mean that it isn't successful."

Both parties consider the status of the arrangement as more than just a supplier/buyer relationship, but hesitate to go as far as to describe it as a partnership. The client observed: "We've got a high degree of trust and a high degree of sharing of information between the two organisations and cordial relationships at a senior level." On the rare occasions when problems have arisen at lower levels, senior managers have easily resolved them.

Most of the work is undertaken on a fixed-price basis with bonuses built into the contract. Bonuses achieved are placed into a pool and are shared by both parties. The relationship has been in place for about four years and the contract is valued at $5million p.a.The relationship has a finite life because the client is gradually replacing the outsourced legacy systems with more modern systems.The amount of work being done by the vendor on the legacy systems is therefore declining and will eventually terminate. Maintenance of the replacement systems will continue.

Implementation

The transfer of 35 client IT employees to the vendor was successful. Employees experienced mixed reactions when told of their transfer to the vendor. Some were excited by the opportunities to progress their careers, work with new technologies, gain exposure to training and increase their skill bases. Others felt a close identification with the client organisation and were reluctant to leave, let alone work for an organisation with which they had no identification. A small group preferred to leave and not work for the vendor and another small number were redeployed within the client organisation. It is now thought that having a formal staff mentoring or people management program in place may have enhanced the transition of employees.The vendor now has such a program in place for all new employees.

The client was concerned about the transition phase because it had to continue running the legacy applications (with the help of the vendor) while purchasing, customising and implementing the new systems. The client was aware of the poor incentive structure for the people who maintained and developed those old systems. They no longer had a future with the client because the vendor now supported these systems. The client describes its outsourcing strategy as: "based around risk management. It wasn't skills. It wasn't costs. It wasn't access to new technologies; it was simply risk. Our relationship with [the vendor] was based on that understanding, by providing our employees with career opportunities post their work here, that we'd be able to protect our position with the old legacy systems. So it was done very deliberately as a risk management strategy". Despite the transition process taking a little longer than expected, the ultimate result has been successful.

The boundaries of the contract are considered clearly specified with adequate service levels having been defined. Because of the difficulty of translating business requirements into software and performance specifications, some ambiguities have arisen, but conflicts have been resolved. An interesting problem can arise when the vendor and client establish a joint team to investigate an issue or resolve a problem. Choosing a team leader from either the vendor or client may bias the recommendations and may be misperceived by client and vendor employees as a win for either the client or vendor.

Successful aspects

Not all clients want continuous innovation nor are they structured to accommodate creativity. However, sometimes the client may not see the ways in which the vendor has developed innovative, creative approaches – rather, the client may only see that the final result stays the same. For all computer systems, even those due to be phased out, there is a constant trickle (or flood) of requests for change triggered by changes in legislation or business. In this case, innovation tended to be negotiated by informal rather than formal means.

In the early stages of the relationship, the client was anxious to eliminate one kind of risk by maintaining access to the employees that had transferred to the vendor in case the service provider failed to fulfil its contractual obligations.

It is interesting to reflect on the factors that made this outsourcing arrangement a success. Both parties enjoy a high level of trust among each other's executives and both agree that the outsourcing arrangement is mutually beneficial. This level of trust is crucial to the smooth running of the relationship.

The client happily gave two examples. "First, both parties have proven their ability to say some fairly abrupt things to each other without in any way injuring the relationship. This demonstrates that we are prepared to talk about all issues. Second, we have reached a point in our relationship where we can discuss potential opportunities for joint business development for the two companies".

The vendor illustrated the level of trust as follows: "They do not scrutinise our bill down to the *nth* degree. But that's because they trust the way we do things and the processes we have in place and any time when questions have come up the accuracy has been spot-on and so that leaves them to feeling the trust of not having to worry about that side of things."

Conclusion

Cultural fit is considered a key success factor. The client feels that the match anticipated from the initial meetings has come to fruition.

The client, although happy with the arrangement, noted the following points that, in retrospect, might have been given more attention:

The client made little use of legal expertise when negotiating the outsourcing arrangement. It is probably prudent to have a lawyer examine a substantial contract ($A5M in this case). One difficulty is that few lawyers are familiar with the fairly new outsourcing paradigm. As noted, outsourcing requires cooperation, but cooperation is an elusive legal concept.

The change was more stressful to staff than had been anticipated and change management processes should have received more attention earlier in the project.

The equally happy vendor noted that:

- The "success factor is being able to perform fixed-price work accurately so it's profitable for us to do and also beneficial to the client..."

- "Another success factor is having the ability to accommodate dramatic fluctuations in the client's business requirements. " It's a major factor in outsourcing that provides the client with flexibility of adapting to workforce requirements that would be very difficult for a client to achieve if the function was in-house."

- A close relationship exists between the employees of the two organisations. "They work very well with each other on projects regardless of who pays their pay cheque... they have one mind of achieving the end goal, not individuals with different priorities."

- The vendor feels that heavily documented outsourcing arrangements have a tendency to become too clinical, resulting in problems with people and processes. Instead, the vendor adopts the philosophy of handling the client work "as if it is our own business, because ultimately it is".

Case 2: ADP Employer Services

http://www.adp.com

The vendor

ADP's core strategy is the provision of a broad range of payroll services and human resource management systems. It performs payroll processing, electronic funds transfer, general ledger posting and mandatory provident fund disbursement, as well as associated print and distribution services. ADP has over 50 years of experience and 450,000 clients, employing 40,000 associates worldwide. More than 33 million employees around the world are paid through ADP's payroll solutions, which are provided in nine languages, across 19 time zones, in 28 countries. ADP has a strong presence in the Australian market, providing payroll services for about 10% of the Australian workforce. ADP has a strategy of expansion into Asia and welcomed the opportunity to gain a large and reputable customer in the Asia-Pacific region.

In Asia-Pacific, ADP Employer Services (ADP ES) – an ADP group company – has been building a reputation in the payroll and human resources industry for over 25 years. ADP ES works with a diverse range of clients, both large and small, in the private and public sectors. Its customer base of more than 7,500 organisations includes many of the region's largest corporations as well as thousands of successful small to medium-sized businesses. ADP ES's partnership approach means that the organisation works with its clients to develop solutions ranging from total outsourcing of the payroll function to the provision of complete in-house payroll and human resource administration systems that are reliable, cost-effective and simple to operate.

ADP's core business comprises:

- Flexible solutions for the delivery of outsourced payroll services ranging from outsource processing to outsourcing of the whole pay office function;
- In-house payroll and human resource systems;
- Management of post-payroll services including interfaces with banks, tax offices and provident/superannuation funds;

- Software customised to reflect customers' needs, organisational size and different kinds of businesses; and
- Facilities management and back-end products that allow employees to access their own information.

During the research program Automatic Data Processing Inc. USA,the world's largest specialist provider of outsourced payroll service and human resource systems, acquired Pay Connect Solutions. This has allowed and encouraged ADP to pursue a more aggressive global strategy and expand its offerings. ADP is now well positioned to leverage its personnel, technical infrastructures and new technologies in moving forward as a global player and realising its vision of becoming the leading provider of payroll services and human resource system across the Asia-Pacific region. This global strategy also incorporates ADP's value-added services and products, for example, salary packaging, employee self-service, electronic payment services, print and distribution services, and employee portal supplements. These ADP services are now available to Asia-Pacific organisations.

The client

The Hong Kong-based client on which this case is based is a leading food and drugstore retailer in the Asia-Pacific region. Its 2,100 outlets are principally supermarkets, hypermarkets, drugstores and convenience stores. At 30 June 2000, the group employed 78,000 people in nine territories; in 1999 it had sales of US$6.8 billion.

Outsourcing is not a traditional business technique in Asia. Asian executives are perhaps more concerned to keep internal processes and data secret. The "jobs for life" tradition conflicts with reducing staff levels by outsourcing. Perhaps increasing competition (especially in technological sectors) and the 1998 Asian meltdown have obliged companies to consider outsourcing as a way of reducing costs.

The client has previous experience with outsourcing non-core activities such as the maintenance of fleet trucks and the installation and maintenance of shop fittings. Its increasing use of subcontracting fits with its preference for outsourcing information systems instead of developing and maintaining them internally. Outsourcing peripheral activities allows the client to focus on improving its core competencies and widening the scope (geographically and functionally) in which its core competencies are applied.

The client's primary driver towards outsourcing was facilitating focus on more strategic HR functions instead of committing resources to the development and maintenance of computerised payroll applications and related activities. The outsourcing arrangement has enhanced overall efficiency by consolidating the six different HR systems that were run by the client into one.

In hindsight, the client feels that a minor motivation was being able to hand over responsibility for the Y2K problem. Although software development and maintenance and Y2K compliance could have been undertaken by the internal IT group, it was better to have the work done by a vendor that specialised in payroll and HR systems. By outsourcing an application common to many businesses, the client can share in economies of scale. For example, ADP could distribute the cost of Y2K compliance and other payroll system enhancements over its many customers.

History

Pre-sales discussions between the two parties began in February 1998. Negotiations and determination of the contract scope took place in June 1998. Implementation began in September 1998 and a three-year contract (with the option to take services back in-house) was formally signed in January 1999. The contract's annual value approximates AUD$1 million and includes a component dependent on the number of transactions.

ADP now performs payroll processing, electronic funds transfer and report distribution for the client. ADP performs about 70% of the client's HR function and provides the following functions and/or services: tailored software (the client has not purchased the licence); payroll processing; access to databases (e.g., those storing employee information); database maintenance; electronic funds transfer to banks; and the disbursement of mandatory provident funds and reports to providers. ADP liaises with the Hong Kong Government to ensure that relevant legislative changes are reflected in the systems. The client is ADP's largest Hong Kong client.

There was no tendering process; the decision to use the selected provider was heavily based on ADP's satisfactory relationship with one of the client's large Australian subsidiaries. This relationship demonstrated ADP's credibility and ADP was keen to enter the Asian market with a large and reputable client. The client wanted to consolidate several different HR systems and ensure Y2K compliance. ADP undertook a business review that demonstrated its ability to streamline the client's processes. The contract was negotiated between equals: neither party had any kind of monopoly power over the other. Top management and general managers of the client's business units were involved at the research stage. Contract development involved IT specialists, general management and legal advisers.

Nature of the relationship

Both parties acknowledge that the commercial reality of their agreement has strong features of supplier/buyer relationship. ADP attributes the status of their relationship to the nature of the business but notes that relationships with the individuals involved are considered more important than any formal description of the relationship. According to the client, the smooth running of the agreement is highly dependent on the quality of the service ADP provides. The client is responsible for keying in the data and ADP is responsible for maintaining and running the computer systems and procedures that ensure that the client and employees receive timely and accurate reports. The critical requirements are for employees' pays and deductions to be correctly calculated, reported and deposited by specified times. Once the requirements had been defined and agreed to, there was comparatively little need for day-to-day discussion; ADP was performing a standardised and routine, albeit critical, task.

A relationship between two business entities can range from strictly arm's length to close and continuing cooperation. Unfortunately, most countries' laws do not recognise cooperation between entities. The cooperation necessary to a successful outsourcing operation, especially the outsourcing of a core function, has no legal basis in Australia and many other countries.

It was not practical to treat this or most outsourcing arrangements as a strictly arm's length relationship. The user's requirements change as business conditions, business plans, volumes of transactions and legislation change. Vendors constantly seek economies and may consequently seek changes in the nature and timing of reports being produced. Both parties may make errors that require programs to be rerun. These circumstances require that vendor and client employees at all levels meet and negotiate, rendering the arm's-length approach inoperable. In this case meetings between one of the client's HR managers and ADP's account manager were scheduled weekly. This assisted in highlighting issues that required more focus and needed to be addressed more formally.

In the early stages the relationship experienced a few teething problems, mainly due to defining and clarifying expectations, but it evolved to became a fruitful working relationship based on mutual trust. Some issues requiring clarification related to ADP's support of the client's staff (the help desk function), not actual payroll processing. ADP observes that better understanding of the division of roles is attributable to clearer documentation of each party's roles and responsibilities. ADP has occasionally performed activities that fall outside the contract on a negotiated-fee basis or, in some circumstances, for free.

A recently implemented example of an innovative practice relates to increasing the client's awareness of ADP's offerings. Although the client is based in Hong Kong, most of the services delivered to the client are performed in Melbourne, Australia. In order to enhance the client's understanding of ADP's services, ADP sponsored the client's account manager to visit ADP's operations in Australia and participate in ADP's User Group. The visit provided an opportunity to build relationships and put faces to names. Moreover, the account manager had the opportunity to build her understanding of ways in which her organisation could use aspects of the system with which she was previously unfamiliar.

Implementation

During the change from internal processing to outsourcing, employees were not transferred to ADP because most of the work is performed in Australia. The roles between the parties were clearly defined from the beginning. The client is responsible for data input and ensuring its accuracy while ADP is responsible for developing, maintaining and running the system, coordinating with the relevant financial institution and printing documentation. Therefore, these tasks did not relate to transferring the client's HR staff to ADP.

ADP was appointed to the conversion project steering committee and acted as project manager. The client notes that one of the critical success factors during the transition process was the importance of good project management practices deployed by ADP. The complexity of project management became apparent as other client departments became involved during the transition phases. Much of the work necessary was performed at a site accommodating both client and ADP employees. This provided opportunities for speeding up the education process and cross-sharing information with people from diverse backgrounds; such discussions prevented small problems from becoming large ones.

The project entailed moving payroll processing from in-house systems to ADP's systems. The client operated six different payroll systems; a subsidiary objective was to operate only one. ADP noted that, as part of transferring applications from in-house to vendor control, vendors often assume the burden of fixing applications and associated procedures that did not work well in-house.

The transition process incorporated three phases over nine months. The technical aspects of this process ensured that people were trained to exploit the new system's capabilities, including extra reports and options. The participation of those contributing to the achievement of milestones was recognised and celebrated, with the client commending the job done by ADP and its staff.

Success factors

The critical success factors for payroll applications are stability and reliability. These are usually static applications and, because they cause disproportionate trouble when they malfunction, a strong case for change to them must be made. Encouragement of innovation and creativity in this function is not a high priority. Both parties have prudently adopted risk minimisation tactics. ADP stores back-up information in two different places. The client monitors the outsourcing market in case the current vendor fails to meet standards specified in the service level agreement.

While cultural fit was not considered a major barrier in this relationship, ADP undertook to ensure that its employees on the project participated in cultural training and briefing sessions. Although the parties are based in Hong Kong and Australia and have different cultures and languages, working relationships between individuals from the parties are good, perhaps because Australia and Hong Kong share a strong enterprise culture. The client described ADP's staff as, "very professional with strong technical expertise... the people are nice, very patient and easy to work with". Most dealings with the client are in English. ADP has employed some local Chinese people who provide the flexibility to talk to client employees in Cantonese.

Communication is crucial as it affects trust between the parties. Importantly, the client has highlighted that communication at the operational level is free and unconstrained. As the relationship evolved prior to ADP establishing its operations in Hong Kong, the client felt that communications could have been improved at the strategic level. With the first phase of the implementation project completed, the account manager was posted to Hong Kong. This posting correctly signalled ADP's commitment and intent (fulfilled in April 2000) to establish a Hong Kong office. An executive has been appointed to Hong Kong and weekly meetings provide the opportunity for both parties to discuss any outstanding matters and provide updates. The regularity of communication is one important component of the large-scale view of the quality of the communication, as is the ability to understand the message being communicated. Still, the cultural difference between the parties has occasionally resulted in misunderstandings. This highlights that greater communication is required in this case due to the different language and differences in local law. ADP is taking care to prevent further misunderstandings: the relationship is not yet routine, and still requires managerial attention.

Conclusion

Both parties feel that the arrangement is successful; ADP provides the services that the client expects at a reasonable price. The client's original goals have been met. For example, four different payroll systems have been consolidated and automated and the client has outsourced a non-core activity. This is consistent with the client's goal of constantly seeking more efficient ways to do business. ADP suggests how the client can improve its process. The software has provided the client with economies and extra information about its business operations; for example, the data in the payroll system can be transferred directly to the client's accounting system.

Cost control

It's a tired old saw, but it remains the case nonetheless: many economies can be achieved by farming out work to specialists who can do it more efficiently. The dominant form of supplier organisation in the cost control mode is the large supplier achieving economy-of-scale efficiencies.

Large-volume, "back office" operations most lend themselves to this scale-based cost-reduction approach. Economies are harder to achieve with smaller operations. The organisations that do this well will benefit a lot in coming years. Those that can crack the distributed model for very efficient service provision to increasingly smaller clients will see the greatest long-term success. Many models argue that it is impossible for one organisation successfully to sell to and serve multiple markets at once[55]. IBM is attempting this with its e-business functions targeted at small and medium enterprises, though it is acknowledging the difference in markets by establishing separate organisation units, styles and locations[56]. Cutting cost via scale-based approaches and addressing cost issues through other, more tailored means, requires keen attention to objectives and method.

One of the cases (**Australia Post Mailroom Solutions**) illustrates this very well. There are other considerations to be made in the circumstance of a pure cost-cutting exercise, of course, and that is to understand the implications for an organisation of changing comfortable reference points. "Improvements" can be unintentionally destructive. For example, the installation of a couple of wells in an African village by a well intentioned Western aid agency improved water access, but it also destroyed a significant element of the social fabric of the community – most of the practical daily communication among the village women was done during the trips to the river to retrieve water. When that time and circumstance were removed, so was an essential element of the cultural infrastructure, albeit in an unforeseen manner. The potential for such situations to develop should be thought through by any organisation contemplating outsourcing.

Cost management can come in other flavours – the avoidance of additional potential costs, for example. Capital costs can be borne by providers in many instances, leaving customers in a favourable balance sheet position. There is also a strong need and desire in most organisations to be able to predict their cost profiles. In fact, a reasonable business plan is impossible without that knowledge. Imagine the frustration of having varying costs from a functional area with marginal capability to deliver. In such a circumstance, it's unlikely that resolution would be achieved without a significant overhaul: either management practices or staff composition would have to change, at the very least.

Case 3: Australia Post: Mailroom Solutions

http://www.auspost.com.au

Introduction

The client in this case is an Australian insurance company.

It is quite common for mailrooms to be considered as back-office, mundane, non-focus service areas. Yet the ramifications of failure to deliver are extremely high, particularly for this insurance company. For instance, failure to deliver can delay incoming payments (usually cheques) and therefore the time taken to process them, which ultimately has an impact on cash flow. Equally adverse is the failure to lodge contracts, which may result in litigation.

An impact on the likelihood of organisations contracting out their mailrooms is the psychological attachment and historical significance some organisations have to these operations. Consider the strategic significance the mailroom has played in screening employees: stories about people that started in the mailroom and worked their way up the hierarchy have almost mythological status. Today such stories, subject to the corporate culture, are less frequent as experience does not play such a key role in advancement as it previously did. We now live in a global economy in which formal education and experience have a greater impact on advancement than experience alone.

Australia Post provides a national postal service, bill payment services (known as POST billpay) for major corporations, and parcel and courier delivery services. Post-on-line represents the latest division within Australia Post (see exclusive case study on Post-on-line's new venture with Coles). The vendor has been a provider of outsourced mailroom solutions for the last seven years. Its experience in handling mail dates back much further, of course. The mailroom solutions division was established through the synergies that could be gained by direct association with the vendor's core business. The types of clients the vendor targets are colloquially described as "paper shufflers": organisations that are required to move and distribute large volumes of documents.

The commercial relationship between Australia Post and the client commenced in 1996 after a long negotiation period. The parties have since renegotiated and renewed a series of two-year contracts without going out to competitive tender. The entire mailroom, courier services and bulk delivery services are the specific functions that are outsourced, over two sites. The client operates in the insurance business and is considered a mainstream type of client – one with high volumes of document movement.

The Internet and the increase in messages sent via email (particularly messages with attached documents) threaten the growth of Australia Post's core business. Growth in Post's core competencies requires a focus on companies that shift a lot of paper, particularly paper that requires a signature or a cheque to be sent through the mail. As method-of-payment options increase as a result of technology, the old saying, "the cheque is in the mail" is no longer guaranteed business. Today, consumers have the option of paying bills via many electronic means. In fact, Australia Post has noticed a significant drop in business-to-business and consumer-to-business mail. The majority of the mail is travelling from business to consumer.

Motives

The decision to outsource the mailroom was one of the first experiences in outsourcing the insurance company had entered into. It was not given a great deal of attention and focus by higher management since it was regarded as just a "back room function". In recent years, this insurance company has become focused on consolidating and contracting out parts of the business. Since adopting this strategy, the company views itself as a more focused service organisation than it previously did. Consequently, greater emphasis has been placed on the infrastructure that supports the service deliveries.

Client: "*We've just restructured and set up a shared services division as our concept of how we're going to manage our business in the future, and supply is now part of shared services. We've outsourced our IT department. I'm presently in the throes of outsourcing our warehouse and office products contract. A whole range of our properties facilities contracts have been reviewed and looked at, parcelling them up, consolidating them and outsourcing them as well as suppliers of all sorts of products. It's all being consolidated and contracted up".*

The client's main influencing factors for outsourcing are costs and efficiency. The strategy emphasised driving down overheads in various divisions. This involved looking to the market to solve cost issues, benchmarking the business and consolidating it.

The client has adopted an encompassing view of the way it views 'costs'. "*Part of the cost is reduction in transactional costs, not just a straight cost of what it's costing us to do something. It's a case of what transactions end-to-end are involved and there are a lot of hidden costs. So we've been identifying our hidden costs and using those as a measure. Service wise – obviously we have an expectation to either maintain or exceed our present levels, and we have to be satisfied that can be achieved within the cost restraint".*

In hindsight, access to skills has also proven an additional motivator. "*I think there's a whole range of issues apart from cost, such as staffing levels, maintaining staff, the overheads of staff and the like. So there's a far more flexible approach by the fact that, if we could offload all that risk and responsibility and ensure that staffing levels were maintained. So the offloading of all those difficulties I guess you could say is one of the big benefits".*

Selection

When the function was outsourced seven years ago, the field of potential service providers was relatively narrow. In fact there were only two major players capable of carrying out the task. The opportunity was discussed with both players in the market and the decision to go with the existing service provider was based on the following factors: the existing relationship; a level of comfort based on the relationship; cultural alignment between the two parties; the vendor's proven ability to deliver; and cost reductions were easy to envision.

Relationship

Gaining the business allowed the supplier to establish itself in the market as a capable supplier of mailroom solutions. The expansion of business into this realm was explicitly part of the vendor's growth strategy. Expanding to a formal commercial relationship was seen as an opportunity to further develop an established relationship. This also fed a high likelihood of success.

This case represents one of the vendor's first external contracts for the described service. This placed them in a very close working relationship from the outset, where they worked together throughout transition and to come up with solutions where relevant. The client acknowledges that the successful running of the relationship is highly reliant on relationship management, and that's how they approach business. The client describes the arrangement as cooperative, yet realises that, at the end of the day: "*Obviously business is business. We have a contract. We expect the service to be delivered and, ultimately, if it isn't, they won't have a contract. It's that simple. By the same token, we don't take a big brother approach. If there are issues to be dealt with, we have a process and procedures in place to ensure that they're dealt with.*"

This arrangement tends to operate with the contract sitting in the bottom drawer – in other words, reference to the contract terms are infrequent.

Strategic planning is driven by the client organisation. The client is willing to inform the supplier of business directions and initiatives that it is undertaking. The main reason for informing the supplier is to give the supplier an opportunity to align itself, if appropriate, with the client.

The areas of business management, financial management, people management and operations are dealt with during a monthly meeting. Analysis of the monthly reports provides statistics such as shifts identified in the level of mail. These meetings provide the vendor with an opportunity to recommend alternatives and deliver solutions according to changes and trends identified in the operation of the business. This may involve rearranging staff between the two sites, according to the volume each site faces.

The contract

The contract is described as very clear-cut and flexible. It outlines SLAs and KPIs that highlight deliverables as required by the client. The clarity of the contract is partially attributed to the total function being outsourced.

The approach to the contract is "let's keep it flexible so it can be a growing, living contract and relationship that allows for the rules to be rewritten when changes arise". The client views the contract as a dynamic foundation that allows appropriate structure to be built upon it as required, but finds that too much contractual detail in the initial stages is a recipe for disaster.

The client's basic rule of thumb in working through the transition phase was to endeavour to capture 80% of major factors/steps/procedures and have a 'safety net' or supporting features to guide the escalation procedures.

The agreement mainly covers current aspects of the relationship and does not explicitly provide processes that allow for future modifications like innovation. When developments or changes arise, they are simply added to the agreement. This is highly dependent on the good working relationship both parties enjoy.

The vendor has contingency back-ups, which are detailed in the contract. A large portion of risk management is based on the relationship and covered by SLAs.

It appears that the newest form of risk management is " keep informed as to who else is out there in the marketplace". The client constantly keeps informed of other players in the market to whom it can move its business if the relationship turns sour. Should that situation occur (breach of contract), the client has the option of exercising the exit clause in the contract that allows it to terminate the arrangement within 30 days.

Transition process

Prior to outsourcing, the mailroom was run by 12 employees. Of these 12, six were employed with the new supplier and six retrenched. Four employees now run the mailroom. The current supervisor was an employee of the client prior to outsourcing. This arrangement is considered quite successful in terms of understanding and knowledge of the client's business. The client considers that the combination of the right skill set and having the right person in the right job has had a positive impact on customer service.

Though there were only two viable competitors, discussions and research took place over a long period prior to the current vendor winning the work. The client spent extensive time scoping out each vendor's capabilities and the synergies that would make the alliance run comfortably.

Both the client and the vendor have experienced, throughout the relationship, change within their respective organisations. The key factor that has kept the relationship running successfully in the midst of change is the flexibility of each organisation to adapt.

The account manager who originally won the work is highly attuned to the client's needs. The client does not hesitate to describe the account manager as passionate about the account and consequently deals with any problems encountered in an extremely swift manner.

Success factors

Throughout the interview the client consistently stressed the importance of the relationship. This is best captured by the following quote:

"Ultimately, it all comes back to relationship management and having a good relationship. And honestly I believe that works in all business. If a relationship isn't working, then you'll find the business isn't working because then there are problems. People become discontented, whether it's from either side, and ultimately that discontent affects the deliverables. So when people are basically happy with the relationship and how they're treated and the way the business is running, then nothing is too much trouble."

In this case both organisations are large, have similar ways of operating and are considered an overall good fit. The client sees the vendor as potentially a large, long-term supplier of services and products.

The vision to establish an environment that is creative and innovative is strongly based on the open flow of communication that exists among parties. Both are willing to share information and develop business-to-business solutions, where applicable.

The cultural fit between the two organisations is described as very successful, so much so that the boundaries between them are difficult to detect. Australia Post staff that work in the mailroom attended the client's Christmas function. The Australia Post account manager uses the following story as an illustration of the cultural alignment between the organisations: "*The client has their own internal magazine, which featured staff from the mailroom. This made them feel like part of the group and a nice little write-up was done about how important they are in what they do*".

Conclusion

The level of service obtained through the outsourcing arrangement is considered higher than it was when the service was provided in-house. This relates to the flexibility the arrangement has allowed. The client purchases the services it requires without having to build and support the infrastructure itself.

The client views the arrangement as enhancing competitive advantage in that it improves its ability to meet customers' expectations. The importance of building a competitive edge in the market, from a service point of view, relies heavily on the service infrastructure in place. This mechanism is also used as the focal avenue for communicating with the client's customers.

A different measure of success is the client's willingness to act as a referee for the vendor when bidding for new business. Word-of-mouth is by far the best advertising. When service levels are such that a vendor is confident that a good referral is forthcoming, then all parties come out ahead.

The client's closing words are: "*It's the relationship management that really makes it work. Ultimately the overall success of what we deliver comes back to the fact that both organisations and the people involved have communicated and developed and worked on delivering a solution. The success has varied over the years – that's seven years – and a lot of it depended on how we have managed our relationship with the vendor and how they have managed the relationship with us*".

Access to skills

Pushing business and accompanying technology to their limits is no mean feat: the limit of technology keeps expanding. The pace of change means that keeping knowledge of technology apace with its capabilities is increasingly difficult. IT workers in particular must constantly upgrade and retrain if they are to be able to push the newest technologies to their limits. Anyone current with the latest technologies, programming languages, development techniques and tools will be extremely marketable and valuable.

Skilled workers have many options. The fact that they are in high demand and short supply means that skilled programmers, for example, can practically name their own price.

In job markets, high demand means high turnover. The cost of replacing a lost worker is about three times the salary of the individual, in general terms, and even more for many IT positions. Opportunity costs, training of new staff, recruitment costs, the costs of retreading old ground with existing staff – these are all elements. The lost time is also a huge loss, beyond the tangible training and other costs. In spite of these well known generalities about turnover, most organisations do not have any realistic picture of the cost of turnover in their own organisations.[57]

In most instances, it is the retention, not the obtaining, of skills that is the most challenging. A recent senior executive survey put attracting and keeping key employees at the top of the list of concerns of CEOs. Marketing and sales positions were described as the most difficult to fill, with IT positions cited as the most difficult to keep filled[58].

The status of skill access urgency varies by placement in the product life cycle. There's a difference between an access to skills that is effectively an employment broker (i.e., simply the details of screening and interviewing, when skills are readily available in the marketplace) and enabling access to what are truly scarce skills. The former will be the case in mature markets, the latter in emerging markets.

IT skills are the most commonly requested and chronically difficult to source due to scarcity. This shortage is affected by the nature of many IT services (i.e., they are intellectually based), innovative approaches and the emergence of Internet-based delivery. True global sourcing is now possible under these conditions. A move toward being "locationally indifferent[59]" will dominate in knowledge-based services. Access to needed skills can happen independent of place.

A green-field example could be one of the best cases to observe – an organisation that was not replacing, but rather effectively hiring (from the outside) an entirely new function. Such is the case with **Hewlett Packard**.

Case 4: Hewlett Packard

http://www.hp.com

The following case is taken from an interview with the HP outsourcing account services manager, and another with two members of the client organisation; one at the strategic level and the other at the day-to-day, account-management level.

About the vendor

Hewlett-Packard, founded in 1939, has long been a leading global provider of computing and imaging solutions and services for business and home. Its basic purpose is to create information products that accelerate the advancement of knowledge and improve the effectiveness of people and organisations.

HP has 88,500 employees worldwide and had total revenue from continuing operations of US$42.4 billion in its 1999 fiscal year. In Australasia, the company was established in 1967 and operates in all Australian mainland states and in New Zealand through its subsidiary Hewlett-Packard (New Zealand) Limited. Revenue generated in Australasia by HP for 1999 was A$1.6 billion.

About the client

The client is a large chemical company that has grown exponentially through acquisition since its establishment in 1970.

Its most recent global acquisition, in 1999, effectively doubled the size of its chemical business in Australia. The new business was purchased without any IT infrastructure or staff. The acquisition forced the company to establish a new IT infrastructure, acquire skills and start building experience in unfamiliar applications in order to support the new $155-million business. All of this had to occur within a challenging implementation timeframe of less than two months, and without disrupting existing operations.

The next challenge was deciding which of the following two options to pursue – outsourcing IT or building in-house IT skills. After a business case analysis led the client to decide not to allocate the resources necessary to build an in-house IT department, outsourcing presented the most viable option. To some extent, the client felt that the decision to outsource was already made, by necessity. The client's general manager noted: "*To transition the IT service of such a major business within such a short timeframe effectively meant that our only option was to outsource. It was a very clear decision: outsource or have no IT*".

The vendor's core line of business centres on the provision of infrastructure outsourcing services, which aligns with the services provided to this client. HP transitioned the client's SAP platform and systems from an RS6000 mainframe to an HPUX platform as part of the outsourcing contract. HP also runs a data centre and a service desk for the client's surfactants business that is staffed from 8am to 6pm, with 24 by 7 remote management from HP's Melbourne operational services centre. HP also provides SAP and Lotus Notes services; Oracle database administration; desktop management; Netware and network management; business recovery; and EDI, faxing and mail gateway services. Application outsourcing is subcontracted to a third party. In this case, the client is most certainly described as a "mainstream" type of client. The supplier saw the potential in this outsourcing deal to further develop its presence in the manufacturing industry.

The contract was signed on 1 October 1999, but interaction between the parties had begun 18 months earlier. The length of current contract is three years with the option to extend it an additional two years. The value of contract started at $1.6 million, has recently grown to $2 million and continues to grow as the services that the vendor offers the client expand.

Motives of the client

The client's principal motivation for outsourcing arose through the purchase of a new business that had no supporting IT infrastructure (such as WAN/LAN service) or skilled staff – hence the urgency in establishing the appropriate infrastructure. The client needed to develop or gain access to expertise in SAP and Notes, which they did not possess, and transition an NT environment to Novell. The client goes on to explain: "*At the same time, we had to support the business processes they had with things we didn't have, skills we didn't have, experience we didn't have, people we didn't have. So we had to outsource. That was the first reason and the most important reason to very quickly get the expertise, resources to continue support for the business. And we achieved that I think very well, very satisfied with the ability to continue to support the business and having IT as an outsource function."*

The client was not motivated by cost saving, as it did not expect to achieve significant cost savings. The client has encountered difficulty in ascertaining whether costs have increased or decreased, or even understanding what the true total costs were. Still, the outsourcing arrangement has provided the client with a greater understanding of its IT costs. Furthermore, the arrangement allows for greater cost efficiencies. These benefits are realised in the way the contract is designed. The contract is based on the concept of Additional Resource Charges (ARCs) and Reduced Resource Charges (RRCs), which increase and decrease the charge unit – whether this is for PCs or people – on a sliding scale. This effectively means that incremental resources over and above the agreed base line cost the client less, thus providing real incentive to grow.

Gaining additional flexibility through accessing the vendor's larger pool of resources also motivated the client. Access to resources has translated into completing projects in shorter timeframes or offering solutions that the client would not have otherwise been able to achieve.

In hindsight, the client believes the overall quality of the service has improved. This is attributed to the vendor's structured way of operating. For example, the level of documentation, monitoring and procedures exceeds the processes the client previously had and is generally accustomed to. The level of activity each month is documented and reviewed during monthly meetings that also provide an opportunity to discuss any issues that have arisen and suggestions to resolve them. These quality improvement tools contribute to overall, long-term systems improvement.

Selection

Once the decision was made to outsource, the client's overseas head office instructed the Australian management to engage external consultants to help drive the process from beginning to end. The client described the vendor selection process as very formal due to guidance by the external consultants. The client initiated a competitive (by invitation) tender process and received 12 Expression of Interest (EOI) responses. The EOI responses were then evaluated and quantitatively analysed according to predetermined criteria. This process identified two service providers that were considered technically capable and showed potential for a strong working relationship. Many intangible factors as well as their ability to understand and address the company's business played an important role in deciding between the final two competing service providers. As explained by the client:

"The way the groups presented, the way they interacted, the confidence they gave you was important... The key thing about the way they present is – how did they prepare, how did they provide the solution, how cooperative were they? These were the specific gut-feel questions that we thought about. Other areas of importance included: could we work with these people, were they the right type, do they substantiate their track record in a convincing manner, what was their technical solution, how will they deal with uncertainty, what was the flexibility they were building into the contract, what was their cost structure like? All of these issues were articulated and responses were analysed."

According to the client, the use of external consultants to manage the tender process placed the competing vendors on as equal a footing as possible. Despite the positive aspects of the use of external advisers throughout the outsourcing process, the client nevertheless voiced criticisms of the consultants. These negative comments were specific to the consultancy firm engaged rather than blanket condemnations regarding the use of professional advisory services. The criticisms were that the client expected the consulting firm to have greater knowledge of the local market, access to more specific material and generic templates. The client also felt that the consultants were too geared to larger, more complex organisations. Despite this constructive criticism, the account manager felt that the client organisation would not have achieved its desired outcomes without the assistance of consultants. The overall view of the client's experience with consultants in the decision to outsource is captured below:

"The use of consultants gave us a lot more confidence and a better footing in the whole negotiations. It was a new area for us. I think we were babes in the wood on this, and people with previous experience enabled us to give a stronger contract. Had we not used them, I think we would have been floundering and would have been taken to town in terms of – you know— our ignorance. So I think it was vital."

Relationship

Client: "*The concept of working in a 'Partnership' – it's a good ideal, but reality is different... fundamentally it's a supplier/buyer relationship...it's very difficult to have a true partnership*".

The client highlights the dichotomy between the client's and vendor's objectives. The client aims to reduce costs and the vendor seeks to make money. This makes it difficult to have a true partnership. Consequently a supplier/buyer type of relationship best describes the reality of this outsourcing arrangement. The client feels that, to some extent, "*it's necessary to have an arm's length relationship... because you have two different businesses and you do require at times to stand apart and sort things out and protect our own interests. So from that point of view we'll never be the true ultimate definition of a partnership*".

The vendor describes the relationship as having "partnering elements." In spite of this, the account manager acknowledges it does not meet the true definition of either a "cooperative arrangement" or a "partnership". However, the aim is to move over time towards a broader, more encompassing relationship. The client states: "*We work together very closely; in fact, I work with them every day. We see them as part of the team and try to maintain a positive working relationship with everyone involved.*"

Organisational reach

At this stage of the relationship the organisational reach is considered a good fit. This is mainly attributed to the relative sizes of the vendor and client. The client mentioned the size of potential service providers as an important criterion in the vendor selection phase. The client is keen to inform the vendor of new business processes, initiatives and direction with the intention of determining areas in which the vendor may be able to assist.

The vendor uses a unit-based pricing model for each service and operates within continuous improvement principles. As the relationship has developed, the vendor has also gained access to the client's costs and budgets for running the business and, where applicable, the vendor assists the client in tasks such as forecasting and budgeting. This sharing of information highlights the trust that has developed between the two parties.

The contract

Both parties view the contract as clearly defined and unambiguous. Yet the client's project manager feels that the contract requires more work, as confusion still exists, particularly when it comes to determining responsibilities. Overall, the contract has many flexible features. The client believes that one of the key benefits of outsourcing IT is the ability to plug-and-patch new businesses into the organisation. This is not normally a consideration with the average outsourcing contract and presented an additional challenge that the vendor has addressed extremely effectively.

Mechanisms exist within the contract for modifications and provisions for new service levels. The client expressed a willingness to 'listen' and explore innovative ways of performing work.

Both parties have adopted some simple strategies to combat problems that may arise from the vendor operating remotely as opposed to on the client's site. The client encourages the IT people in the vendor organisation to do some of the support work; so employees that work at the help desk are invited to visit the sites and talk to the client's employees. The client also organises visits for the managers of the businesses to observe the vendor sites. They also rotate meetings between vendor and client sites. The client noted: "*We try and understand that there are people there and that there are people here and we want them to see that. So even though people don't work here from HP, they have certainly visited and we keep encouraging them to do that.*"

Transition process

The transition process was heavily driven by meeting the cutover date for transferring the new business – hence the system had to be fully enabled before the deadline. Despite time constraints, the vendor successfully met this deadline. The outsourcing contract was signed on 3 October 1999; it was a requirement that the IT services be fully transitioned by 1 December 1999. HP shared exposure with the client for business disruption costs of up to $150,000 that would have been applied if the transition had not been achieved on time. Effective project management skills and the vendor's experience contributed to the successful transition process. No employees were transferred in this case; the vendor's employees service the client remotely.

Phases in the outsourcing process

The client's main grievance throughout the outsourcing process was the small size of the vendor's team. Consisting only of an IT manager, a contract manager and a technical manager, the team was felt to be too intense.

The client considered the use of legal expertise throughout the process as crucial to its success.

The vendor felt that not enough credence was paid to change management and communication issues. The vendor states that: "*We didn't realise the extent of the impact that the changes were going to have on the users. This resulted in the users feeling a loss of autonomy, which subsequently led to a series of aggravated calls logged at the help desk.*"

The vendor has developed and regularly updates relevant cocumentation pertaining to the client. The vendor has employed a strategy of cross-skilling to ensure ongoing access to the necessary skills. This involves a portion of the vendor's employees possessing functional knowledge of the client's requirements/operations while another portion is considered "experts" on the client. The account manager, on the vendor side, seeks to create a positive image of the account by holding workshop/training sessions with employees. One of the objectives of the sessions is to create an atmosphere in which employees come up with solutions, not just problems.

Customer satisfaction surveys and performance reviews of service level metrics are undertaken monthly.

Success factors

Both parties acknowledge that although their respective organisations' cultures are quite distinct, this has not affected their working relationship. Both parties consider the management of the relationship more crucial in ensuring its success than the cultural fit between the organisations. The ability to compromise and for "both parties to come to the table" appeared to be a common theme suggested by all parties interviewed.

The major variable that affects the acceptance and implementation of creative or innovative processes is cost constraints. Hence, the majority of creative processes tend to be cost-saving initiatives.

The client believes that the right combination of commitment, dedication and resources devoted to making the arrangement work has led to its success.

Conclusion

Both parties believe that clearly understanding and articulating what one wants are the foundations of success. The client considered the vendor's ability to demonstrate how it would deliver what it had as an important selection criterion. It is recommended that the sales team should represent a combination of operational people who understand how a service is delivered and sales/marketing people. This is to ensure congruence between what a vendor promises to deliver and what it is actually capable of delivering.

The lessons learned from this particular arrangement are:

- maintain regular meetings and open communication channels;
- solve problems together; and
- foster a positive attitude among all team members of wanting to work together.

Doing it better

Though not always the initial justification for entering into an external sourcing arrangement, an improvement in quality of services delivered is the most visceral and beneficial outcome. There are several variations to the "doing it better" theme: higher quality, faster turnaround, more flexibility, leveraging skills. Each of these has a varying effect on organisational metrics and performance, and therefore varying effects on their perceived benefit as outgrowths of outsourcing.

There are parallels in the introductions of many technologies. The introduction of PCs in organisations is one with which most of us are familiar. PC proliferation was often justified based on promises of productivity improvement. Though these improvements may have been achieved in many cases, the benefit did not always fall to the bottom line of organisations, and much PC spending was soon seen as wasteful[60]. A more accurate assessment is that the benefits weren't anticipated, articulated or captured. This same challenge faces outsourcing teams as they work to identify and capture the very real benefits of improved quality of service.

The case of **Programmed Maintenance Services Limited** is one in which service quality was a primary driver and benefit. The **Hansen** case demonstrates 'doing it better' by leveraging skills through the vendor's client focus and service culture.

Case 5: Programmed Maintenance Services Limited

http://www.pmsltd.com.au

Background

The following case is taken from two interviews, the first with the deputy principal of an independent Melbourne school. He has personally been involved in this relationship for one and a half years. The deputy principal is responsible for enrolments, scholarships and the school's development and presentation, which is considered crucial in maintaining the image of the school. The second interview was conducted with the Manager of the Engineering Division at Programmed Maintenance Services (PMS); he was instrumental in getting the arrangement under way and currently oversees the relationship as the account manager. This case deals with the outsourcing of the school's property maintenance activities.

The business of Programmed Maintenance Services Limited was established in 1951 in Victoria, Australia, as a commercial painting contractor. PMS pioneered and developed the 'programmed maintenance' concept in the late 1950s and has since established a dominant market share in its core painting business in Australia and New Zealand. PMS has also expanded its maintenance philosophy into a range of related service areas. In recent years, PMS has expanded its range of property-related services to include grounds management; building and engineering services; specialised drainage, sewer and plumbing services; and a national corporate imaging service. PMS now offers a comprehensive spectrum of integrated services to its customers. PMS's business philosophy centres on providing first-rate property maintenance services, using its system of long-term maintenance as well as traditional 'one-off' contracts.

PMS does not see itself as a facility manager, it provides a package of trade-based, maintenance and property management services to a number of its customers. Over 30% of the vendor's client base operates in the education industry, including many large independent schools in Australia. PMS provides a different range of services to schools, dependent on their specific internal requirements and 'cultural' values. PMS believes that no one outsourcing model is applicable to every school.

School facilities are considered an essential part of the educational environment. All buildings require some level of maintenance to ensure they are functional and meet safety standards. The condition of a school's buildings and equipment may affect how students and teachers perform, adversely impair curricula and potentially affect the number of enrolments, particularly in today's competitive climate. In Melbourne, strong competition drives the industry, which in turn affects the behaviour and strategy many private schools adopt in relation to maintenance.

Facilities maintenance of the school property covers a wide collection of activities from breakdown or damage to facilities or equipment, through routine servicing, minor replacement, major repairs and rejuvenations, to refurbishments, replacements and ultimately demolition with the intention to rebuild. A portion of the maintenance work falls under the category of planned maintenance. This covers areas such as routine servicing, replacement, refurbishment and overall upgrade of facilities. The other portion takes into consideration unplanned maintenance responsibilities.

In the past, the client had an in-house maintenance team that performed the day-to-day maintenance of the school facilities. This arrangement was becoming problematic, particularly in relation to delivering to the quality and standard the school expected. As distinct from the in-house facilities maintenance team and their responsibilities, painting services have long been farmed out to various contractors. Three years ago, PMS began providing external painting services for the client. PMS identified other services it could offer the client and alternative ways of managing the school's facilities, which would ultimately improve the presentation of the school grounds. In order to implement these new management strategies, the client and PMS decided to introduce a PMS employee to manage the existing facilities maintenance team for a trial period of six months. The existing team did not respond well to the changes being introduced. Following the trial period, the client decided to totally outsource the facilities maintenance function to PMS.

In May 1999 a formal contract was signed that detailed the outsourcing of the day-to-day maintenance of the school. This consists of an on-site maintenance manager with two maintenance employees. A three-year contract with a fixed base value of $100,000 per annum is in place. In addition, a six-year painting contract is also in place between the parties. The decision to go with PMS mainly hinged on the existing relationship that had been established through the external painting arrangement and PMS's role in providing a facilities maintenance manager.

Motives of the client

A strong impetus for outsourcing arose from the client's dissatisfaction with its existing arrangement. Hence, the client sought to improve the quality of services provided and general productivity. The secondary driver to outsource was to gain access to a larger pool of resources that could provide additional flexibility to accommodate the school's ongoing requirements. This is particularly applicable to ad hoc projects that may involve coordinating and managing a wide array of tradespeople.

The client was not driven by cost savings, but rather motivated by achieving value for money. The client considers that its current arrangement provided greater value for money in comparison to the previous in-house arrangement. The client supports this in stating: "*This has been achieved with one less staff member, compared to in-house, and tasks are accomplished in a shorter timeframe*".

Relationship

In essence the arrangement has features of a supplier/buyer relationship, particularly when the client requests additional staff for ad hoc projects. Despite this, both parties feel that elements in their relationship indicate a cooperative or partnership-style arrangement.

The client views the relationship as a cooperative arrangement and attributes this to two main variables. First, the flexibility provided by PMS accommodates the peaks and troughs in the work level required by the client. Second, the maintenance team closely identifies with the school even though they are employed by PMS and wear its uniforms. The client considers that this close identification and affiliation with the school enhances the overall quality of the service. In fact, the client prefers that facilities maintenance team members are not rotated through other schools and that instead they continue to grow as a team.

Both parties consider their relationship to be straightforward and honest and this is reflected in their contract. In fact, the process adopted in developing the contract further reiterates this; both parties established the outcomes the client wanted to achieve and allocated the necessary resources to optimally achieve this.

Monthly meetings between the relevant individuals provide an opportunity to discuss targets that have been reached and outstanding jobs and timelines. These meetings also provide an opportunity to discuss ideas and potential changes to the existing contract.

Evidence exists of the vendor providing services that are beyond its contractual obligations. The vendor has an open price policy with the client and frequently assists the client in budget preparation and estimates in costing a facilities-type of project. In addition, the client seeks the vendors' advice on new buildings and landscaping ideas, even for projects that the vendor is not contracted to execute.

The contract

As indicated earlier, the contract is considered flexible, clear, well structured and well organised. This is attributed to the process adopted in developing the contract. In essence, PMS has a contractual obligation to ensure that the school complies with safety regulations. This involves meeting the relevant statutory standards and ensuring sign-off when compliance has been fulfilled.

This case is an example of SLAs forming a live document and the client preferring to keep a close watch on agreements that were negotiated. The main reason for this is to ensure that the contract continues to accommodate the school's requirements.

Processes for suggesting and implementing changes or innovations in the work being performed under the agreement are in place and initiated by both parties. The vendor has proven to be flexible, fair and willing to alter some of the specifications in the contract. For example, a certain amount of money is allocated to painting the exterior of the school's buildings. The exterior was still in good condition and not ready to be re-painted. Discussions led to the money allocated for exterior painting being used to paint some classroom interiors.

Transition process

The transition process was handled successfully due to the vendors' previous experience and knowledge of the client's requirements. A notable improvement in quality and overall efficiency has been observed in the maintenance service. A success factor is the maintenance team's enthusiasm and willingness to complete tasks. The only misstep in the process was administrative. This is a common issue during the transition phrase as the relationship is moving through untested waters and heavy documentation is required.

Success factors

The client ranked the following as successful: operational procedures, management practices, cultural fit, problem handling/resolution, level of trust and encouragement of creativity/innovation. According to the client, administrative processes related to documenting quotes and/or alterations could be further enhanced. The existing process involves completing a Request for Maintenance (RFM) form, which goes to the maintenance manager. The work is effectively processed and actioned in the nominated timeframe. Emergency maintenance requests are taken by phone to ensure best-practice response.

The right team

A great deal of effort went into selecting a team whose members complement each other, in terms of both personality and skill set. This is seen as a positive force in the smooth running of the relationship. This also applies to replacement employees who are used when members of the regular maintenance team are on leave.

The current team demonstrates enthusiasm about their work and their outputs, which has resulted in an increase in productivity. They have demonstrated a willingness to complete tasks rather than question the rationale behind why the initiator wanted the task performed in a particular manner – an issue with the client's previous maintenance team.

Skilled resources

The client's ability to tap into a multi-skilled organisation was considered as one of the crucial factors to the success of the outsourcing experience. The vendor provides ongoing access to necessary skills, by providing training courses to all of its employees. This reinforces their value in the workforce. The courses PMS offer cover a vast array of topics from front line management, to computer skills, to obtaining scaffolding licences, to safe work practices and occupational health and safety.

Relationships

Strong relationships between the client and PMS have had a positive impact throughout the contract. For instance, both parties worked together in establishing expected outcomes from the outset of the arrangement and monitor the expectations of meeting the stated outcomes. Setting such outcomes from the beginning has played a significant role in measuring the success of the arrangement.

Conclusion

Since inception, this arrangement has proven successful. Goals have been met as measured by the improved quality of the service and productivity in comparison to in-house standards. It is believed that these benefits have been transferred to the client base, consisting of teachers and students, through the provision of safer facilities. Frustration arising from managing a facilities maintenance team has been relieved, allowing employees at the client organisation to concentrate on other areas.

The private school market in Melbourne is regarded as highly competitive.The client believes that the quality of the school grounds leaves a positive brand image on potential students and their parents, thus contributing to competitive advantage. In addition, well presented school grounds and facilities are easier (and generally less expensive) to maintain than replace. This translates into additional funds being allocated to educational requirements rather than upkeep of the school grounds.

In summary, the key success factors in this relationship are:

- achievement of goals within timeframes;
- option to tap into the a multi-skilled organisation; and
- strong foundations of a flexible relationship.

Case 6: Hansen

http://www.hancorp.com

The following case is taken from two interviews, the first with the client's Manager of Information Systems. The second interview was conducted with the account manager and the business development manager at Hansen Corporation.

The vendor

Since its inception in 1971, Hansen Corporation has supplied integrated information systems and services to the Australian market. The Melbourne-based company also has operations in New Zealand, the UK and North America to support its international client base in the public and private sectors across various industries. Hansen focuses its activities on four key services: customised billing and customer care solutions for the telecommunications and utility (electricity, gas and water) industries; IT outsourcing and facilities management solutions; software and services for workforce management; and infrastructure asset management systems.

Hansen delivers tailored IT outsourcing services at all levels – from the management of a single system or a couple of support services to total IT outsourcing. Its IT outsourcing services include: facilities management services; systems and operational support; network services; call centres; telecommunication equipment housing and support; and business continuity.

The client

The client organisation (a statutory authority) is a rural water authority, created in 1994 as a result of a state government water reform program. The client covers major water storage facilities and the major gravity irrigation areas in the state as well as pumped irrigation and waterworks districts. It provides rural water and drainage services to approximately 24,000 properties. Its responsibilities include: management of the major water systems within its boundaries; provision of bulk supplies to (non-metropolitan) urban and rural water authorities; and delivery of irrigation water, domestic and stock supplies, and drainage services. In addition, the client undertakes a number of natural resource management activities, finance, engineering, irrigation farming, water systems and environmental management.

In 1994 the state government began a program to reform its water industry with the objectives of increasing efficiency, maximising benefit to customers and reducing the state's debt burden. These public sector reforms have resulted in the restructuring of the capital city's metropolitan water industry. The water industry covers rural, metropolitan and non-metropolitan urban sectors of the state. All water businesses are owned by the state government and pay annual dividends through the treasurer, who acts as shareholder.

The state's Water Industry Association is its top water industry organisation. It represents the government-owned water businesses in the state. These businesses consist of three metropolitan retail companies, 15 non-metropolitan urban authorities and four rural water authorities. The Association works with member businesses and with government to influence policy and practice that affect the state's water industry.

Background

Prior to this outsourcing arrangement, the client received its IT services through a 35-person subsidiary company. The client was not wholly satisfied due to low perceived value in the arrangement; in 1997, the c ient decided to spin off its subsidiary unit. The subsidiary IT company was thus acquired by Hansen in February, 1998.

Hansen had an established relationship with the client prior to the IT deal, providing workforce management services. With the new acquisition and outsourcing arrangement, the specific IT services that Hansen now provides the client include: help desk (first- and second-level support); desktop support; problem and change management; networks; software development (business systems and DBA); technical support (Unix, NT); Internet service provision; project management; and some hardware support. The length of the current contract is three years (valued at $3.2 million) plus a one-year extension (valued at $900,000).

The client has one other major outsourcing service provider, in the area of distribution planning.

Motives of the client

The client's primary driver in deciding to outsource was to reduce costs via the more efficient shared resources of a larger IT provider. This driver arose from inconsistency and lack of transparency in costs from the previous supplier (the subsidiary IT company). The level of inconsistency in costs significantly affected the client's ability to manage the business effectively. Predictability of cost, together with economies of scale from a larger provider, was seen as a potent combination for achieving cost reductions.

Cost reduction was viewed as attainable through the economies of shared resources, not through the capital cost avoidance that often accompanies an organisational divestiture. The client had already spent the capital (or at least committed to it) and has no plans to change from the current model, in which it owns the IT infrastructure.

A secondary motive was to establish a fully commercial relationship that could be market-tested. Having made the decision to break the ties between the client company and its IT subsidiary, a transition to an autonomous, viable and self-sustaining commercial entity was necessary. This transition is a complex and difficult one for most spin-off organisations. For the client, the relationship with Hansen is the cornerstone upon which the spun-off entity's viability was built.

Selection

The selection of the vendor was accomplished through a tendering process. Third-party assistance was employed in arriving at a short list and evaluating the tenders. Given that the client wanted to divest its IT subsidiary, it was necessary to choose a vendor that was both willing and able to take on the staff and provide the services with the desired results. In part because of the staff transfer requirements, the vendor selection process included (in addition to third-party assistance from consultants and legal advisers) a wide range of internal management expertise. Strategic, legal, account management and financial experts from the client were involved.

Motives of the supplier

Part of Hansen's expansion strategy involves growth by acquisition. Hansen's acquisition of the client's IT subsidiary took place in 1998, but its commercial relationship with the client dates back further. Hansen began providing payroll services for the client in 1996. The primary motive for Hansen was to exploit a niche opportunity in providing and expanding on IT outsourcing services in the non-metropolitan regions of this state. To date, only small local firms provide such IT support, usually at an increased cost. Using Hansen's central metropolitan infrastructure, regional communities can take advantage of economies of scale in certain operational areas such as Help Desk and Server Management.

Relationship

Both parties felt the arrangement was reached on an "equal footing" basis – there was mutual advantage in the situation (expansion by acquisition and niche market opportunity for providing regional IT services for the vendor; increased capacity, expertise and economy for the client). There were no obvious advantages held by either party, making for a straightforward negotiation process.

The client sees the relationship as a standard supplier/buyer type of arrangement. The services are operational in nature and do not require the more complex arrangements of a partnership or strategic alliance. Hansen's organisational reach is considered appropriate and the relationship allows for the vendor to provide input into strategic decisions where suitable.

While some aspects of the service requirement, and thus the relationship, have changed over time, the intention all along on behalf of both parties has been to develop a cooperative relationship. The client and the vendor feel they have achieved this, with the vendor describing the current situation as "symbiotic". This sort of subtle evolution is not unusual in IT outsourcing.

The contract

Both parties describe the contract as very detailed with clearly defined boundaries and satisfactory SLAs in place. Operational people were involved in contract and SLA development.

Regular meetings provide the forum to review SLAs, issues that may have risen and relevant provisions for change. SLAs are reviewed in detail annually, with no external mediation. Employees are encouraged to look for alternative ways of undertaking tasks. This method of SLA management protects the client by ensuring service levels are maintained without being restrictive. The arrangement therefore enables any client business changes that require modifications in IT services to be reflected in the services provided.

No formal risk mitigation or disaster recovery agreement is in place. The client handles potential risk through liability insurance, and through the option of exiting the contract should service delivery fail.

The client considers some targeted increase in insourcing as an option if performance slips below an acceptable level or when it ceases to be a viable business option. Significant software development projects and high-level technical skills are not considered likely targets for insourcing.

The vendor cites two illustrative examples of how the view of mutual benefit and innovative approaches have helped shape a successful contracting arrangement:

"Insourcing, or the allocation of service to another vendor, really boils down to the client's perception of value from the service delivered and the competencies and capabilities of the vendor to deliver the service (see section entitled "Clarification of Value Proposal"). If the vendor cannot add value to the service being delivered, then the cost of that service should be passed through. If it is not, then the client might as well insource.

"To this end, innovative practices have been put in place benefiting both parties. The first example involves a network response bottleneck with a subordinate regional site that faced increased bandwidth requirements from expanding staff

and IT needs. This site was also paying more than necessary for ISP. The client is now working with Hansen to implement a radio-based telecommunications link that will provide more economical access to high-speed Internet services, with the savings funding the new link.

"Equally instructive and illustrative of 'thinking outside the box' to deliver a solution of mutual value was that of service delivery at one of the client's subordinate sites. Staff at the second largest of the client's subordinate sites perceived that they were receiving an inferior service with respect to desktop support due to the lack of on-site representation, even though the original contracts did not call for dedicated on-site support. The client lacked the budget to increase the site's level of support and management was unsure about the level of support required. However, as Hansen was supplying the service, the internal overheads in managing complaints from the site were rising to such a level that a proactive response was required to stop the increase of the vendor's own costs. In assessing the logistics of site visits made to all of the client's regional sites, Hansen dedicated an on-site resource to provide the local support required without the need to vary the cost, term or conditions of the existing contract. The vendor also improved its margin through reduced overheads by way of complaints to the Help Desk."

Transition process

The transition was described by the client as "invisible, with no disruption to business". It is an odd situation to strive for – in effect, no impact – but that is what an effective transition achieves. Seeming effortlessness requires much effort, of course, and that effort usually entails generous amounts of planning and commitment. According to the client, this is precisely what happened: *"Overall the transition was positive, very well planned and executed ... the right people were involved in the right stages." "The vendor displayed speed and flexibility throughout the process."*

Hansen took on all the staff previously employed in the subsidiary IT company. The vendor recognises that its key asset is its skill base and spends a lot of effort developing its people to ensure they have ongoing access to necessary skills. Some of the strategies employed by the vendor to ensure constant individual growth involve cross-skilling and rotation. Acquisition of skills is a significant success element from Hansen's perspective because these skills improve Hansen's capability and broaden its service offering. The client wins by receiving a reduced price point for the provision of certain skills that, in its previous service arrangement, would have cost an entire person rather than part of a resource as they do now. The vendor wins because it picks up those skills and redeploys them to another client.

Such a smooth transition is not always the case, however, either for the vendor or the client. Just as there have been many client war stories about poor outsourcing transitions, vendors can also put themselves at risk. In one instance in which Hansen acquired a company rather than won a specific contract, more staff than were expected left due to dissatisfaction with the exiting incumbent management. In this case Hansen has had to allow for an increase in the transition cost through increased wages to retain staff. Therefore, for new business that Hansen wants to win, the vendor always ensures that sufficient staff are available to manage this change, both on a business and a technical front.

This preparation had a positive impact in this case, as the client felt that the level of management expertise adopted throughout the phases of the outsourcing process was effective. There was a clear understanding that the different phases of a transition to outsourcing require different types of capability. Hansen uses formal project management procedures that detail planning processes and risk mitigation through the transition. Legal expertise and financial management were heavily involved throughout the phases of outsourcing management in this example since Hansen was dealing with a company transfer as well as functional outsourcing.

Success factors

Both parties feel a high level of trust exists in the arrangement. The client feels that a higher level of trusts exists in comparison with its previous provider, particularly regarding pricing. There was not an open-book pricing arrangement with the previous supplier and the client was unsure about whether it was receiving value for money. One of the most influential factors in the establishment of trust in any kind of commercial relationship is a history with the other party. The fact that the vendor had an existing relationship, and therefore a history, via its workforce management services, increased the trust levels.

Both parties rank the degree of cultural fit as high, attributing it to previous history, the close working relationship and openness. From a Hansen perspective, cultural fit is normally aligned with the type of business it seeks. Hansen strives for outsourcing business in the second-tier market, usually utility-related, where clients are looking for flexible, low-cost solutions.

The typical approach of a smaller support group (such as the 35-person IT group in the client) is to provide services in a relatively informal, personalised and reactive fashion. A larger support organisation, supporting a larger customer base, necessarily takes a more deliberate and highly managed approach to problem handling and service provision. The transition of the smaller group into Hansen has resulted in a more sophisticated problem handling and resolution process than was available from the previous provider. A more detailed escalation process is now in place, which has had a positive impact on the speed of resolution, thus enhancing the process.

Conclusion

The client describes the "old IT department" (the subsidiary) as "*somewhat out of control. In hindsight, we were trying to get rid of a problem by selling the subsidiary*".

The client considers the standard of services to be better now than with the subsidiary firm due to the following factors: quality of resources; scalability of services; greater accountability; greater transparency and predictability of costs; and an overall reduction in costs.

The client considers the arrangement to be successful overall. The client has singled out several specific factors as major contributors:

- The vendor has demonstrated flexibility in service provision – for example, expansion from payroll services to IT services, and flexibility in options for the range of service provided. There is an increased flexibility in staffing now – staff can be shifted, for example, as needs arise, and there is greater ability to serve remote locations.

- An open-book approach has proven especially successful in this situation. Resourcing, inputs, costing and pricing are all done transparently and are therefore understood and accepted, or intelligently negotiated.

- The quality of service provided has demonstrably increased. This is due in part to getting the expertise you pay for: competent people are available to solve problems. Another major contributor to quality levels is the delivery of solutions that are tailored rather than pre-packaged and standardised.

- Previous history of service and an established relationship have created a high degree of trust.

Ultimately, the customer/vendor relationship depends upon the understanding and expectation of that relationship for both parties. Both participants must want to succeed by working together, either at the transactional level at one extreme, or at the partnership level at the other.

The vendor's perspective on what makes outsourcing arrangements successful includes the following general points.

People: The new challenge for the delivery of IT services is maintaining an environment dynamic enough to retain staff. This can be done through cross-training and cross-skilling employees across differing projects and clients to enable them to achieve higher satisfaction levels.

Open business strategy: Hansen maintains independent relationships with all major IT vendors in order to provide an in-depth, specialised service. Although Hansen provides consulting regarding IT decision-making, its clients tend to make their own decisions on IT strategy while Hansen focuses on implementation. This experience has been born out in this case.

Clarification of the value proposition: Hansen identifies services in two categories: non-value-added and value-added. Non-value-added services include third-party supply or any service to which Hansen provides little or no added value. Hansen maintains an "open pricing" policy in fulfilling such services, disclosing the actual value to the client and passing it on at cost plus a small accounting fee. Hansen views value-added services as those of which Hansen itself maintains a supply or property and from which the client will receive value.

Service culture: Hansen's service culture is founded on the principle of removing technological angst from business issues. It seeks to achieve this goal for its clients through cost minimisation without sacrifice of quality or delivery of service.

Price: Hansen is economically focused on delivering services at their highest potential value. It maintains a "tight ship" policy on cost control, managing marketing, employment, operational expenses and financial control in detail.

Focus on core competencies

Core competencies are not products or things we do relatively well; they are activities – usually intellectually based service activities or systems – that the company performs better than any other enterprise. They are the sets of skills and systems that a company does at "best-in-world" levels and through which a company creates uniquely high value for customers.

Developing best-in-world capabilities is crucial in designing a core competency strategy. Unless the company is best-in-world (including transaction costs) at an activity – whether within a function or inter-functionally – it is another organisation's core competency, not its own, and the company gives up competitive edge by not buying that skill from a best-in-world source. A best-in-world target forces the company (1) to think clearly and explicitly about strategic advantage and (2) to look laterally at other enterprises not in its own industry when seeking performance comparisons and improvements.[61]

Intellectual- or service-based competencies – like product design, software or maintenance – can be acquired from any external source in the world, whether a specialist "boutique" firm, a consulting firm or an integrated company seeking to leverage a specialised knowledge group's skills within its own integrated value chain (as FedEx sells its logistics management or telephone answering services to others). For a variety of reasons including tradition, emotion, and incapacity or unwillingness to evaluate internal transaction costs and risks objectively, companies may continue to perform many uneconomic activities in-house. But in doing so they suffer unnecessary costs and risks for not buying the activity from best-in-world providers.

Seeking best-in-world performance offers powerful recruiting, motivational and innovative benefits. The best people want to work for the best company – hence Intel, Lucent or Sony can attract better personnel for their core competencies than can competitors for whom such activities are peripheral. Once on board, such people find "distinctive leadership" a more attractive target than being "among the best" companies in the industry[62]. Being best is a target that creates identity, cohesion and emotional satisfaction for talented people. No successful coach or battle commander ever takes the attitude that "tomorrow we will be one of the two best teams on the field." The very act of defining "best" and actively seeking "winning" performance creates a clarity of purpose and unifying challenge that allows clearer delegation to small, self-motivated innovation groups, engenders much higher creative responses from them and forces consideration of a wider range of options than benchmarking – i.e., just matching the best. Benchmarking can merely ensure competitive parity or mediocrity, not being best at anything.

Once a company develops a true best-in-world core competency, it never outsources it and may even build defensive rings of essential competencies that customers insist it have or that protect its core – as Honda does by not outsourcing design, parts or key equipment for its core competency, the design and manufacture of clean, efficient small engines. Other than its core and essential competencies, most companies can reap great gains by prioritised outsourcing of many activities for which they are less than best-in-world. If a firm is not best-in-world at an activity (including transaction cost) and continues to perform that activity in-house, it gives away a competitive edge that it could have exploited.[63]

Upon serious investigation, most companies will find that 60 percent to 90 percent of their in-house activities are services that are neither being performed at best-in-world levels nor contributing significantly to competitive edge – and are not very risky to outsource. These should be the first targets for analysis.

The profound strategic decisions around keeping or divesting a competency is the centre of the cases of **Atos Origin** and **T-Systems.**

Case 7: Atos Origin

http://www.atosorigin.com

The following case is taken from two interviews, the first with the General Manager of IT Shared Services from the client organisation, a publicly owned Australian chemical company. He was a member of the steering committee and has personally been involved since the inception of the arrangement as a vendor manager. The second interview was conducted with the account manager at Atos Origin.

Background

In 1999, a publicly owned Australian chemical company decided to divest its data centre and mid-frame operations in order to focus on its core business. Access to technology was also a key driver of the outsourcing decision. The specific functions outsourced include: data centre, mainframe and mid-range operations, and some network monitoring services. The client has four main business areas – mining services, agricultural chemicals, consumer products and chemicals.

Atos and Origin merged on 31 October, 2000. The combined entity has a high skill base of 27,000 employees that operate in 33 countries, with sales of EUR 2.8 billion in 1999. Atos Origin's core business is to provide value to clients by helping solve their business problems with enabling technologies. Atos Origin's business focus is on understanding their clients' business and providing customised design, build and run solutions with speed and efficiency. They achieve this through their global capabilities in the following IT services: consulting; enterprise solutions; application and infrastructure management; and data processing together with systems development, implementation, integration and management. Their industry sector expertise covers high-tech manufacturing, chemicals and pharmaceuticals, retail, consumer-packaged goods, and banking and finance.

At the time of writing, the parties were 18 months into their three-year contract and have a two-year extension option. The contract is valued at $35 million over five years. About 24 staff members were transferred from the client to the provider as part of the arrangement. This IT outsourcing contract is the largest arrangement that the client has had with external providers. Other functions that the client has outsourced include auditing (internal and external) and facilities management.

Expression of Interest (EOI) responses were sought from 12 vendors, of which four were short-listed and progressed to final due diligence. Responses came mainly from tier-two players. External consultants were used to help drive the decision-making process. They assisted in establishing the RFI, the RFQ, the tender responses and contract negotiation. The client felt that it was essential that external expertise be brought in to help with the process and establish a framework, as this was the first large IT outsourcing contract that the client had experienced. The evaluation process is described as a formal process of detailed tables of weightings, assessments and measurements.

The experience with the external consultants resulted in the client organisation establishing a supplier/management framework that was developed during the process. This framework is used on an ongoing basis with any external supplier that the client does business with, regardless of the size of the contractual arrangement.

Selection

According to the client, several critical factors led to Atos Origin winning the business. The most important was Atos Origin's ability to take on the client's staff at equivalent or better terms and conditions, particularly those relating to the provision of similar or enhanced career opportunities for employees who had transferred across. Assessing the vendor's culture was crucial in determining the appropriate fit. The client expressed these points in the following quote:

"The culture of the company was a crucial component of the selection process. We analysed the legal terms and conditions of employment, where they were going to transfer all of our staff and what sort of assurances they had, that they're actually going to be there for an extended period with career planning and training and so on. We didn't want to transfer all the staff and within a month find they'd all been sacked. We discussed such issues during negotiations and built them into the contract."

Secondly, the client considered it critical that the chosen service provider possess the global strength to support the client with potential expansion of service offerings to accommodate the client's offshore operations. The third factor was the analysis of the financials that mainly comprised the building and the provision of the services. The fourth feature the client sought was the expertise to provide additional services – for example in SAP and e-business – as potential future services that the client may require. The client has already started to take advantage of some of the additional services that Atos Origin has to offer, such as e-business services.

The client organisation had no previous history with the service provider in Australia; however, the client's international offices did have some experience with the service provider.

Both parties agree that the arrangement was reached on an equal footing. The client particularly felt that: "*the external consultant that was used was invaluable in helping set the sorts of criteria that we needed to carefully manage and carefully control – plus our knowledge of our data centre and the cost structure and the services made it invaluable, and us being able to sit at the negotiating table and be able to challenge some of the outsourcers' assertions about their ability to deliver cost savings and added value. Because we've been there and done that and we knew that they either were or were not achievable. They weren't able to pull the wool over our eyes*".

Relationship

The relationship, at this point, is described at the supplier/buyer level with evidence of moving to a more cooperative arrangement. As the parties move out of the transition phase, the supplier has greater flexibility in coming up with new ideas and ways of doing things.

The client's view of the concept of partnership is captured below:

"*The concept of 'Partnership' within outsourcing has the tendency to be a throw-away line that a lot of people use and don't really understand what it means. To me, a partnership is when each side is prepared, as we say, "to put a bit of skin in the game". That is, a partnership is where each side is contributing and sharing the risk, sharing the cost of coming up with innovative ideas and jointly benefiting from benefits. In a customer/supplier arrangement, nobody wants to share the risk; therefore, they bump the margins up and make sure the prices are right."*

The client provides some evidence that may indicate that the tendency to scrutinise pricing models and/or invoices is behaviour indicative of supplier/buyer relationships.

"Every time we ask Atos Origin that we would like a new service or a changed service, very clearly they have a process of how to handle it. And I think that it was in the early days – it's still a little bit of lack of trust because we would scrutinise the pricing models and come up and say, 'well that's too high, we know you can get a better discount rate for that sort of equipment. You know your margins are too high there'. So we were scrutinising at a very detailed level. So it's very much the supplier/customer focus. We are now getting to the point, I believe, where there's a bit of trust being developed and we're now not scrutinising the numbers so much because we know the sort of ball park and Atos Origin knows that we understand the pricing and can sort of validate that any time in the marketplace. So I think we're moving up the scale."

Organisational reach

The organisational reach is on a technical/operational level because of the nature of the operation of a data centre and provision of technical services. According to the client, there have been some tentative discussions about expanding the scope of services offered. However, the vendor's ability to provide services to meet the client's current requirements generally falls into that technical/operational category at this stage. At quarterly high-level strategy meetings held with Atos Origin, both parties share events that are occurring within the respective organisations to identify if there are synergies and new ways forward. Atos Origin has successfully completed many projects outside of the original contracted scope over the last 18 months enabling the client to take advantage of different services, skill sets and knowledge from the one source. These capabilities assist the client in addressing its evolving business requirements.

The contract

According to the client, the critical part of the negotiations involved defining service level agreements. This process was considered time-consuming and involved a lot of work to reach an acceptable level of clarity. He goes on to say, "*once the contract is signed, it's very much implementing the transition of those services, and we have what we call a master controlling document, which is several large volumes, and it is a working document that defines roles, responsibilities, service provision interfaces, change control, all of those aspects*". In the early days, during the transition, there was a degree of uncertainty, as would be expected as the staff who transferred to the service provider were used to doing things for the client. A portion of the transferred employees' tasks stayed with the client and the other portion went to Atos Origin. The transition period involved a significant portion of time to adjust and settle into the new roles.

It is agreed among the participants that a static contract that remains unchanged for three or five years is simply not realistic. The client recalls that changes started occurring almost on the day the contract was signed. The client acknowledges that the critical aspects that require up-front confirmation during the contract negotiations include: scope variations, the contract variation process and the pricing methodology. Getting these components right allows new employees that become involved in the arrangement (post-contract negotiation) to understand how the contract operates.

There are processes in place for implementing changes upon receipt of a client's request for a new service. This process documents details such as specifications, price, revised service levels and the like, thus ensuring the clarity of the service being requested. The relationship is still at a point where the parties are too focused on ensuring that the transition establishes the correct foundations to direct their energies toward the problem of delivering creative and innovative solutions. Both parties are confident that in time this will change.

A value-added component exists in the agreement. The vendor considers the challenging component to be establishing a relationship close enough to allow them to understand exactly what the client considers valuable. Otherwise innovative ways of doing business that are of no interest may be presented to the client.

The contract has service failure adjustments (SFA) in place, so if a certain service level agreements or performance criterion is not met, fees are adjusted accordingly. There are also provisions in the contract that stipulate that repeated failure to meet services may invoke heavier penalties. The contract has limited scope for allowing for rewards or bonuses; however, it may be expanded in the future. According to the client, another way of managing risks is through the short contract period: three years is very short in the scheme of outsourcing.

Transition process

The transition process took longer than expected due to complexity and the amount of work required as well as delays from both parties. Understaffing from both parties also encouraged extension of the transition period.

The mix of expertise was considered effective throughout the phases of outsourcing. Particular attention was paid to the HR/change management process through the various phases. Very intensive communication also kept all employees informed of changes.

Success factors

Both parties ranked operational procedures as successful; ultimately the same people are doing the same job. Cultural fit is considered very successful. Cultural fit, positively handling the staff transfer and trying to move towards a partnering arrangement that centres on trust and openness were the key criteria in selecting the service provider.

Trust takes time to build and develop and both parties feel that it is growing. The client compares the varying levels of trust in the following quote: "*I would have said it was less six months ago than it is now. In six months time, it will probably be more than that. And that's just going to be evolving as the relationship matures.*"

Conclusion

The client sees the arrangement as successful since its goal of getting out of the data centre and mainframe business has been achieved.

The client's view of success factors is captured in the four points below:

1. Be clear about what you're outsourcing. Understand the costs, services and potential disruptions in addition to the reason why you're outsourcing.

2. Put considerable effort into the negotiation process, including identifying and addressing SLAs, pricing formulas, change management and flexibility.

3. Break the legal component into two. First, attend to the actual clause – its description, relevant penalties, risk and so forth. Second, consider the intent of the clause – what do you want to achieve? How can this clause achieve this?

4. Identify a service provider that possesses cultural similarities.

The vendor's perspective on the key to success in this relationship is twofold:

1. Develop a deeper understanding of the client's broader business needs to ensure the appropriate perspective is applied.
2. Continually work towards strengthening the relationship so that the customer is valued as an integral part of the team.

Case 8: T-Systems

www.t-systems.com.au

T-Systems was formerly known as debis IT Services.

The following case is taken from an interview with the Chief Information Officer of DaimlerChrysler Australia/Pacific (the client in this case), and another with the Managing Director and Senior Manager of the debis IT Services Australia/Pacific team. All interviewees had been involved with the outsourcing arrangement in question from the time debis IT broke away from DaimlerChrysler to form a separate entity.

Since the interview took place, debis IT services merged with AST Consulting. This merger has provided a core capability that extends Australia-wide with offices in Melbourne, Sydney, Brisbane and Perth. More recently debis IT Services became part of the Deutsche Telecom group, with IT service revenues in excess of Euro 11billion, 38,000 employees and representation in 23 countries. The global brand is know known as T-Systems.

Introduction

T-Systems has performed as one of Europe's leading information technology service providers since 1990. Part-owned by Deutsche Telecom and DaimlerChrysler, T-Systems works to plan, build and run IT solutions for clients seeking competitive advantage in their respective fields. Worldwide, the former debis IT Services portion of T-Systems now generates more than three quarters of its revenue from operations in over 20 countries external to its parent, the DaimlerChrysler Group.

In Australia, T-Systems (and its debis IT Services predecessor) has operated as a discrete entity since it separated from DaimlerChrysler in September 1999. Previously, the organisation functioned as part of an internal IT service department handling build-and-run functions within DaimlerChrysler Australia/Pacific, supporting the organisation's custodial responsibilities towards its local subsidiary brands.

The T-Systems/DaimlerChrysler outsourcing arrangement is unique within this collection of case studies. As an offshoot of DaimlerChrysler (itself the product of recently merged giants Daimler-Benz and Chrysler), T-Systems has an unusually intimate understanding of the client organisation's operations.

In early 1999, a decision was made to detach part of the knowledge-rich IT services department of the recently rebadged DaimlerChrysler group. This positioned T-Systems to develop its core line of business and more adequately address the needs of external clients, while allowing DaimlerChrysler the freedom to concentrate on the role of developing strategy for local operations.

T-Systems' core line of business in Australia pursues the conceptual framework laid down by one of its international founding partner, debis Systemhaus: Plan, Build, Run. In Australia T-Systems may work with client organisations to strategise information technology operations, plan projects and build information systems, but in its role as service provider to DaimlerChrysler the "build" and "run" service components are most important – the client continues to develop strategy and plan internally.

As a result of the decision to develop T-Systems external to, but as a subsidiary of, the DaimlerChrysler operation, one sees an unusually high degree of interplay between the two organisations as they carry out their outsourcing arrangement. In fact, no formal contract has yet been signed to set down the terms of their arrangement – this document is still under development.

DaimlerChrysler in Australia holds an outsourcing arrangement with IBM GSA, and has released other non-IT functions, including cafeteria, cleaning and offices supply services, to external providers.

Motives of the vendor and the client

The major influencing factor behind the decision to form T-Systems predecessor, debis IT Services, into a new entity was the opportunity the move provided the former IT services division to generate new business with external clients. The move was aimed at better using the skills base of the IT department and generating a more profitable operation. Client: "*That was really the main driver. There was a corporate board behind it".*

As part of the agreement made at the time IT services were detached, the new debis IT Services was given the assurance that it would carry part of DaimlerChrysler's IT workload for a period. Thus, there was no open tender – the usual presales interaction did not occur. Although DaimlerChrysler has reserved the right to seek new service providers after the initial period, its time limit has yet to be formally determined. At the moment, the client assumes a three-year agreement.

Relationship and reach

This outsourcing arrangement is characterised by a unique relationship between client and service provider. Because of the client-owned status of the service provider, it seems neither party is greatly concerned by lack of a signed contract at this stage, although the service provider acknowledges the growing need for one. For the time being both parties appear to rely heavily on their close working relationship as they work towards developing mutually beneficial outcomes. This is indicated, to an extent, by the reluctance of the parties to set a time limit on their agreement – they acknowledge in this way that, during T-Systems formative years, things may change.

Some members of the service provider's team were employed by the client for well over a decade. Service Provider: "*I'd have to say that we're a partnership because of the relationship and the past history – in its true sense, rather than what some external vendors say to a new client. We want to be a partnership – a partnership's not just words, and it comes about through the strength of the employees that were outsourced and the relationship they have with other people – the users inside the business. So I think we would say it's a very strong partnership, rather that just a partnership, and I don't see it moving that far away from there.*"

The client and service provider entered their agreement on an equal footing. Client: "*We knew exactly how things were running internally and we both had our ideas how it should be changed, and from that point of view we started from the same basis. He (the service provider) knew exactly what I wanted to achieve internally, and he had his plans how to set up his group to help us to achieve that."*

There are benefits to the apparently strong relationship between client and service provider. For example, there is "*support and advice and information on issues that we share in a partnership, rather than just telling somebody that's what we need. We can discuss solutions and options and so there is additional service involved*".

The contract

A formal signed contract has not yet been produced. While a contract that addresses the concerns of all parties is being drafted, interim documents describe important standards for operation, including service levels and desired outcomes. All parties agree that the role of each is clearly defined and understood. External legal consultants have been engaged to draft formal documentation to define the outsourcing agreement.

Even at this stage there is evidence that, due to the nature of the relationship between parties, any formal agreement will be developed and modified over time to the benefit of those involved. Regular, high-level meetings occur between client and service provider to encourage a flow of information. Account managers and liaison staff work toward this same goal.

High-level discussions are also taking place to evaluate the inclusion of shared-risk-based components in the final documentation. These might include service level bonuses and penalties. Draft documents also contain transition arrangements for early termination.

Transition process

The transition process in this case was somewhat complex. Considering the enormity of the change involved in part of DaimlerChrysler's IT department becoming a separate organisation, the transition was smooth and well managed. The move to detach the IT staff into a separate group was a gradual process. At first, only the name of their operating unit changed – they continued to use the same offices alongside their old DaimlerChrysler colleagues. Over time, T-Systems located an interim office. Moving into new premises gave the new entity a firmer corporate identity – being in the old building had, as the service provider notes: "*made it virtually impossible for any of those long-term employees (there's a couple in the 15-years-plus range) to conceive that, just because they had a new name, that anything had changed. So it's really since we moved (to the interim location) for the majority of staff that they've recognised that they're an employee of [T-Systems] – because they're not having what was literally minute-by-minute contact with the client.*"

The change to a new location has also been evident in service outcomes. Initially, with established working relationships so firmly entrenched, it was difficult for staff to move from their employee mindset to a service provision paradigm. With the benefit of distance, the service provider observes: "*the process has become very clean and oriented around service since we've moved here. Once we were physically separated and there was a clear delineation of who's who – it was very straightforward.*"

The client found that its outsourcing model, which saw build-and-run functions handed over to T-Systems, was particularly suited to its unique situation. Client: "*What worked well was to take on the build-and-run business based on the fact that people basically continued to do what they had been doing before. In our case it was not really a difficult thing.*" The client also acknowledges the benefit of moving T-Systems to another location: "*It helped them to work in a more formal relationship with us rather than being part of an internal department. We also had to think about formal processes – how we work together – and that has already created improvement in the service delivery even without a formal contract.*"

T-Systems' staff initially consisted of former DaimlerChrysler employees who transferred to the new operation when their interim agreement took effect. T-Systems has since expanded its skill set through external hiring and mergers

Phases in the outsourcing process

The outsourcing process is still under way, with formal documentation under review. Change management expertise was employed to control the transition phase. Legal consultants have been engaged to draft formal documentation. It's admitted that some problems might have been tackled differently: Service Provider: "*I'd definitely appoint a person as a full-time project manager to actually work though all of the transition issues and build a project team beneath that as needed for the particular circumstances. I see it as giving a dedicated resource to DaimlerChrysler as our client – to give them a focus, rather than the scattergun approach they sometimes get from us because we come from the internal."*

Success factors

The service provider and the client consider several factors critical to the success of this outsourcing arrangement. All of these factors are aspects of clear, careful management of the relationship and the attendant expectations.

Strong management

The need for strong management was raised as a factor critical to the success of any operation undergoing significant change. The service provider, in this case, has indicated that at times it was forced to remedy problems from an operational perspective, rather than a managerial or strategic perspective: Service Provider: "*Our management has been extremely light and therefore not 100% focussed when the inevitable has arisen*".

Culture

Both parties have raised the need for a strong corporate culture and identity. Each reports that when T-Systems staff came to see themselves as a separate entity responsible for providing a service to its client, rather than just another wheel in a much larger machine, service levels improved.

Relationships

Strong interpersonal relationships between client and service provider staff are seen as both a positive and negative force. As a positive force, the strong relationships between upper management staff on both sides of the partnership have aided a complex and risky transition process. The level of trust exhibited on both sides has allowed the arrangement to develop naturally over time, rather than as a prescribed affair laid down in legal documents. As a negative force, the strong relationships between staff made the transition a slower process than it might otherwise have been – it was not until T-Systems moved into its own offices that the service provider paradigm really developed.

Documentation

Both parties have indicated that more concrete documentation might have improved the transition process, and that a signed contract that clearly outlines service level outcomes and other goals is a necessity now that the two organisations are moving further apart.

Conclusion

The T-Systems/DaimlerChrysler service arrangement has proven successful over its first 18 months. Service levels are improving as new systems for managing the interaction of the two parties are implemented. Parties to the arrangement exhibit a knowledge of and alignment with the goals of their partner. The flexible nature of the current arrangement has seen a degree of change take place in both organisations – thus far the learning curve has not proven too steep.

To reiterate what makes this particular arrangement work well:

- Strong relationships;
- Regular meeting and open communication between parties; and
- Service provider's depth of knowledge regarding client operations and objectives.

Sharing the risk

Some might call it a case of having no other options, but one of the most compelling reasons to engage in an outsourcing arrangement is to backfill a critical capability that you simply can't do on your own. This is a very different arrangement, when not outsourcing means not doing the business at all. Most early-stage products and services are at that point. Offerings that have not yet matured to the point of a full end-to-end offering necessitate cooperative arrangements. Most of the New Economy companies boast of the number of alliances and strategic partnerships they are engaged in as much as one would expect to hear bragging about the number of customers or sales the company has. New products and services demand access to a wider range of capabilities than most organisations have at the ready

This is true not only for young, New Economy start-ups with relatively few resources. Large, established organisations looking to continue to see themselves listed as such in 10 years' time must do the same things. The following case study illustrates exactly that circumstance. Two decidedly Old Economy organisations have identified business opportunities that take advantage of New Economy trends. They also recognise that, in spite of substantial resources, they are better off sharing opportunities -- and risks -- with an organisation well-suited and complementary.

Hence the partnership of Australia Post's groceriesonline and Coles Myer for online grocery services. These two organisations have put considerable time, effort, expertise and resource into an enterprise that has yet to turn a profit. They recognise the upside and downside potential and are pursuing them together.

Case 9: POST groceriesonline DELIVERY

Australia Post, the country's primary postal operator, provides a mail and package delivery service that handles 4.8 billion items every year. The organisation employees 35,397 people, operates 4,479 retail outlets nationwide and covers a total of 8.8 million delivery points[64]. Post's services have extended beyond traditional delivery services; retail and financial services, including banking and bill payment, are now part of the package offered at local post offices.

Considering the extent of Post's presence within the customer and delivery service sectors, it is little surprise that the mail carrier sought and successfully acquired an arrangement with Coles when the grocery seller moved to augment its 431[65] stores by commencing online sales. The following case, based on an interview with John Raphael, National Manager POST groceriesonline DELIVERY, and Rob Gray, Group Manager Business Strategy, outlines Post's strategic realignment.

Background

Australian Post's primary business – letters – is susceptible to both substitution and a falling economy; mail volume is a very quick indicator of economic growth. With the rise in use of the Internet as a means of communication and transaction, Post has become vulnerable to a shift from paper-based interaction to cheaper and faster electronic methods. Web-based billing and payment systems, for example, are a direct substitute for, and therefore a threat to, Post's core business.

In recognition of this, Post has extended its efforts to incorporate three distinct strategic thrusts within its overall business plan. One of those thrusts is to extend and defend letters, the organisation's core line of business.

In Australia, the ratio of transactional mail to promotional mail is approximately 85 to 15. In other developed economies overseas, the ratio is closer to 50-50. This presents both an opportunity and a threat to Post: the organisation depends heavily on transactional mail, which is vulnerable to substitution. The opportunity, however, is that Post can drive promotional mail services harder and achieve new growth. In Australia, while every man, woman and child receives around 23 pieces of promotional mail per year, Europeans average about 80 and in the USA the average is closer to 400 pieces. Post sees potential for much growth in this area.

The second strategic thrust laid out by Post's corporate plan stems from its expertise in letter mail. Over time, the organisation has developed significant core competencies in database management. These present opportunities for Post as a provider of services, subject to strict privacy arrangements, like mailing lists, surveys and an array of market research products. These, in turn, are services that may well foster growth in the promotional direct mail sector, above.

The third major component in Post's strategy has been developed in response to a question asked by the organisation's planners: how can Post leverage its core competencies – network management, financial skills and the like – and move into other market sectors? What stands out very firmly is logistics management: "after all, it's very hard to substitute a parcel electronically. Until we can say 'beam me up, Scotty', it's going to be a bit difficult" *(Gray)*.

Looking overseas, a single trend is most obvious. The German Post Office, one of the most successful in the world with 30% floated last year, has seen a shift over the past 10 years. While last decade perhaps 80% of the organisation's revenue came from letters, now the proportion is less than a quarter. It has moved into parcels, logistics management and financial services. Similarly, the Dutch Post Office and a number of other post offices around the developed world have experienced a similar shift.

The trend towards logistics represents an opportunity for Post. It already has the necessary skills – fleet management, scheduling and route optimisation, and the like. Post recognised that it was "only a short step and a jump from network management for letters and standard parcels"*(Gray)* to network management that incorporated the logistics needs of a third party.

Coles Myer Ltd

As the largest retailing group in Australia, Coles has a strategic imperative to defend and retain business. Coles recognises that to ignore the growth of the Internet as a tool for commercial transaction would be to open the door to competition. As a consequence, it would lose some of the security that its position as market leader affords it. Further, it would forego a potential growth opportunity.

John Raphael, as Post's Relationship Manager for Coles Myer Ltd, recognised Coles' need and saw an opportunity to match his organisation's strategic core competencies with the supermarket chain's strategic requirements. Provoked by a long-time interest in e-commerce and its effect on the supply chain, Raphael went to work with his colleagues to put together a marketing paper, a high-consumables delivery business proposal, which leveraged Post's expertise in delivery.

Raphael credits Post's recognition of the importance of customer relationship management as the key to the organisation's successful engagement with Coles. Rather than the salesperson's approach of seeking new ways of selling old products, Post actively sought opportunities to work together with its customer.

"*Post has an exceptionally good relationship management programme. At the top level we have what we call Corporate Account Executives. They are well-paid, senior people in the business that look after our biggest customers. Then there are tiers of sales people at different levels, managing different sized relationships.*

That was how we identified, if you like, this electronic retailing initiative at Coles and tried to put ourselves in the frame, leveraging off the very things that we do very well. If we didn't have a relationship, we would have been on the same playing field as everyone else. And, I'd like to think that, although at the end of the day it did go out to tender, we were in a much better position than anyone else." (Raphael).

Australia Post spent around eight months preparing the tender for the Coles project. Raphael drew on KPMG Consulting as a source of supply chain management expertise, along with a number of internal people. "It is fair to say that is was a very substantial investment for us"*(Raphael).*

Ultimately, Post won the tender to provide Coles Online with logistic support. The arrangement is non-exclusive – other supermarkets or retailers may take advantage of the new operation, groceriesonline Deliveries. A trial commenced, initially in Victoria, which later expanded to include New South Wales.

groceriesonline

Shopping at Coles Online is simple. Individuals visit the supermarket's web site and make their product selections from the offers available. When they have completed their shopping, they proceed to the checkout, supplying delivery details. At this time, between three and five delivery "windows" will be offered throughout the day depending on their location. As these windows fill, they drop off the list of available timeslots.

"This is a challenge for us. It's a phenomenal challenge. I spend a lot of time looking at numbers. I'm not sure we understand any of them yet, because it is very difficult to work out the rhyme and reason [while still collecting] the data. Why is it that one day is spread evenly and demand the next day is polarized, and how do we go about meeting those needs?" (Raphael).

The service costs less than $14. While individual reasons for using the service vary, groceriesonline's customers are largely time-poor. They perceive significant value in paying the nominal fee to have someone pick, pack and deliver their shopping within a two-hour window.

"No one's making any money out of this business yet. The efficiencies that come with volume will change that, but frankly, it costs a lot more money than is being charged for in the great scheme of things to pick, pack and deliver those goods"(Raphael).

No online payment facility exists at present. Payment is taken at the door on delivery via mobile EFTPOS. For this reason, Post has spent time re-evaluating the presentation of its drivers and trucks. The vehicles used will be strongly branded with Coles Online to help grow the supermarket's, and in turn Post's, business.

"*We will do what we can do to enhance the image of Coles Online as much as Post, because at the end of the day, the key cost driver for us is delivery density. The more customers we have, the more cost-effective we become. These people aren't just delivering to a letterbox. They're knocking on people's doors, they're asking them to hand over their credit cards. They're carrying out a transaction using mobile EFTPOS in front of the customer. They're often entering the home*"*(Raphael).*

The vehicle itself is significant; it is a new design specifically developed by the project team to serve the particular requirements of the task at hand. It has three separate temperature zones. While other trucks are refrigerated, none are designed to make more than a few stops a day. The new groceriesonline truck can handle multiple stops and the door repeatedly opening.

"*It's had a lot of testing with the CSIRO Food Sciences Australia to make sure that it meets the Australian Cold Chain Code of Conduct, and not only that, but the future standards that I'm sure will be imposed upon us, which are the current European standards for cold chain management. A lot of thought and development has gone into it. It is a unique vehicle. We've built a prototype, and we will be going out to tender*"*(Raphael).*

Raphael and Gray are surprised at the amount of press that the groceriesonline project has generated both internally and externally. "It's amazing that what is in the great scheme of things a relatively small fish in the great ocean of Australia Post, how much interest there is – a tremendous amount of press"*(Raphael).* While Post runs a fleet of 6,000 vehicles, groceriesonline is expected to account for perhaps 150 trucks within five years.

Challenges

Groceriesonline will face a number of problems as the service is developed further. Post has identified two issues of some concern to the operation.

In a time-critical business like delivery, small delays can add up to large losses. For Post, time at the dock and time at the door are crucial factors in the operation's efficiency.

"If we ask for goods to be ready at a certain time and they're not, then that has a very substantial impact on my business. Not only are we not out there earning revenue for delivery, but we're also delivering late, and then I require extra resources to cover the fact that our truck has been tied up"(Raphael).

Accepting payment has been another hurdle. Post's drivers have been trained extensively to handle the new mobile EFTPOS equipment, but delay is inevitable.

"Time at the door is one of the issues that we've considered. Now, to deliver and perhaps get a signature and leave is a different matter than asking for the customer's credit card, swiping it, getting the access to the bank, keying in amounts and saving or cheque, producing a receipt, having the customer sign for it. That takes time, and we know that time equals money. So, there is a cost for that, and the cost is several minutes in time"(Raphael).

Demand uncertainty presents another significant challenge to Post. In these early days there is limited data to allow planners time to develop an understanding of the behaviour of the market.

"I've spent a lot of time analysing numbers, only to come to the conclusion that I don't have enough data. On a given day we find that the delivery windows that are filling are polarized early morning-late night, which is not the unexpected. But then, the very next day, they seem to be evenly spread through the day, which, of course, is ideal for me because I get to use my resources evenly right through the day. So, that's still a challenge I am working on, frankly, trying to understand that. What's the difference between a Monday and a Friday and why is it so? What's

the difference between a pay week and a non-pay week? These are all things that we're investigating together with Coles"(Raphael).

Success factors

Post has identified three factors that have been, and will continue to be, critical to the success of the groceriesonline project. First, the trust the public places in the Australia Post brand and in the organisation's experience in delivering to the householder gives Post a sustainable advantage over others that are keen to move into the industry. This has become particularly important in the groceriesonline case. The role of drivers has shifted from the traditional and task-oriented to a customer service role; they interact with customers, taking payment and receiving feedback.

"So, what did Coles see in us? Well, I think they saw a number of things. One is our experience and expertise in residential delivery, I think the strength of the Post brand. Post is an extremely well recognized brand in the marketplace and very well considered. And, we're talking about things that are very different. We're talking about delivering to people between the hours of 6.30 in the morning when it's dark until 9.30 at night when it's dark, and they don't want Joe Bloggs' courier company knocking on their door. They feel a lot more comfortable when they see the Post-branded vehicle pulling up out in front and the Post delivery driver knock on their door"(Raphael).

Second, Post relies on its dominance of the 'last mile' – the benefit of the widespread coverage that gives them access to 8.8 million separate delivery points.

"When you're delivering many millions of pieces of mail a day, you'd have to say that logistically Post are way out in front of all of our competitors. We own what's typically called the 'last mile'. And we do own it. Our competitors, particularly in parcel distribution, are strong in the business-to-business market. When it comes to putting their fleets into residential areas they fall over badly. So, [Coles Online] was residential delivery and we're very good at residential delivery. We're extremely good at residential delivery"(Raphael).

Third, Post recognises that leverage of its experience in logistics is critical to success. Further, the development of real-time planning will move Post well beyond the competition. The planning tools that provided an efficient means of clearing street post boxes, post offices and licensed post offices provided a basis. Groceriesonline has taken that a step further for the Coles Online project, using Post's vast experience in logistics to provide a more dynamic and flexible solution. The next step, dynamic route optimisation, will see routes planned in real-time while trucks are in the field.

"Today, we take a data file from Coles. We sort that into the most economical delivery and we tell Coles to pick it and pack it in that order. We load our truck and it goes off and delivers in that manner. So, the truck is scheduled to within minutes of its life right throughout the day. 'This is exactly what you'll do and this is how long it should all take'. Dynamic route optimisation is the ability to throw other things into the task, but once the vehicle is loaded, there would be other things – the pick-up of the dry cleaning, the drop-in at the video shop and delivery of those things. I won't go as far as to say hot pizzas yet. I just spent a lot of money on refrigerated trucks. But, all of those things are potentially where we might go with dynamic route optimisation"(Raphael).

Moving forward

Australia Post's trial with Coles Online has concluded successfully: Post is now Coles' carrier of choice wherever Coles Online opens around Australia.

"Is there anything that I'd do differently? I don't think so. Does that sound terribly smug? Timelines — I wonder, would I have stretched them out a bit? Perhaps, but if you don't put your timelines up and if they're not a bit ambitious, then, you know people keep taking the soft option. So, maybe I would have said there were some things like customer interface, IT interfaces that have taken a bit longer than I would have hoped, and cost Coles a lot more money than they would have hoped, but in the great scheme of things, I'm very happy with the way it's going.

We, as a corporation, worked hard on this. I've been involved with fleet management for many, many years. I can tell you, never have I seen the amount of effort that's gone into us building a solution for this customer. I've never seen anything like it. We have done the numbers. We are deadly serious about it and we've had some good consultants as well along the way, and we have lots of our own people here with skills in delivery to leverage from"(Raphael).

References

[55]*Moore, Geoffrey, "Crossing the chasm" op.cit.*

[56]*Levitch, Gerald, "Not your father's IBM", Report on Business Magazine, April 2001*

[57]*Mosley and Hurley, op.cit.*

[58]*William H. Mercer/Angus Reid poll, Toronto, 1999.*

[59]*Harrison, Russell, op.cit.*

[60]*Hurley, Margaret, Managing the Desktop: Delivering Business Capability, Nolan Norton Institute, Melbourne, 1997*

[61]*Quinn, James Brian, "Strategic outsourcing: Leveraging knowledge capabilities", Sloan Management Review, 1999, 40, 4.*

[62]*ibid*

[63]*ibid*

[64]*Figures as of 1999-2000. Employment figure includes 26,915 full time and 8,482 part time staff. See http://www.auspost.com.au/mediacentre/index.asp?link_id=4.6*

[65]*See http://www.coles.com.au/about_us/company_info.htm*

Chapter Five

SKILLS - THE KEY ASSET

It is sometimes forgotten, in the day-to-day management of business, that the only real asset in most outsourcing arrangements is the collection of individuals who execute the terms of the agreement day to day. For vendors of outsourcing services, this is absolutely crucial, far more important in most instances than the supporting technologies or processes, which are rendered useless without that staff. For the buyers of outsourced services, there is an implicit admittance that they are either unwilling or unable to acquire and manage the personnel required to do the jobs outlined in the outsourcing agreement. So, the starting premise here is that keeping a cadre of qualified people is important to the company, though an outsourcer may more efficiently provide those people.

There is a sense among many managers that human resource issues are "soft" and difficult to define and manage, enmeshed as they are with personal preferences and wide variability. It is not unusual for these issues to be shunted aside as a result, to be put in the "later" pile and somehow to end up being deemed relatively unimportant as a management topic. This is common, and a big mistake. It's precisely because of its "softness" that it's so hard. In comparison to areas where metrics and processes are well defined and proven effective, much of the management of the people asset is just a hard slog.

It's a hard slog and hard economics – economics that are rarely scrutinised. The majority of managers with personnel responsibility do not know and have never even guessed at the costs of turnover[66]. Basic facts such as salary are known. Managers generally have an astute, intuitive sense of the emotional toll that staff turnover has on those remaining in the organisation. But the full picture of the effects of employee turnover is poorly articulated and even more poorly measured.

This is beginning to change, of necessity. Outsourcing arrangements are one manifestation of the tipping of the balance regarding management of the human asset in an organisation. While one organisation explicitly offloads the responsibility, another takes it on as the centre of its success. In the same way that a successful manufacturing organisation understands its supply chain and material sources, a successful service provider understands the sources and uses of its people's knowledge and skills.

The type and availability of skilled people is influenced in large measure by market conditions. Since the mid-1990s, many areas of information technology skill have been chronically difficult to staff. For example, in North America, the shortage of qualified IT professionals is so acute that federal governments have intervened and allowed qualified IT professionals from any country to enter work (as non-immigrants) in North America for three to six years without requirement of a specific job offer. This is in addition to all other immigration allowances. The US H-1B visa program is planning to add 300,000 such visas over the next three years, above the more than 200,000 already admitted[67]. Regional shortages of health care professionals are also a long-standing challenge – nursing has been at the top of the "skills wanted" list for immigrants into the US, UK, Canada and Australia for decades[68]. (The US H1-A visa for non-immigrant nurses predates the IT industry's H1-B visa.) The approach to and viability of filling any position must consider these factors – cost and availability top the list of considerations.

In addition to immigration, skills are being shipped abroad. Organisations are now emerging that will broker IT skills, particularly with developing-world sources such as India, Israel, Ireland or Malaysia. Such brokers typically receive between US$1,500 and US$5,000 per person for finding the right IT skills for a US- or European-based business. These brokers are based in both sending and receiving countries, monitoring and responding to market conditions. The trade in skills is so brisk that it can accommodate virtually any situation as conditions warrant. Everything -- from offshore, over-the-transom style work, with workers based in the country of origin, to coding "sweatshops" of new immigrants, to IT-based versions of the American Dream – is being done now, and will continue as long as the skills situation stays this way. There is also a brisk trade in skill futures – if you know that a large project will need a certain type of skill in eight months and don't want to take the risk that you'll be unable to find those skills at the time you need them, then there are organisations that will take the risk for you, for a price. You pay a premium now; they'll find the skills then, locking in availability for you.

Along with the skill brokers, in the developed world, some of the top programmers actually have agents (just like Hollywood stars). This indicates the level of market desperation and the highly negotiable nature of compensation and conditions at the top end of the skill spectrum. This will continue as long as there remains a shortage of skill. Seeing a lucrative opportunity, many people will train for these top jobs, alleviating the shortage to some degree. The specific jobs at the top of the skills-wanted heap may change as a result. But as long as IT usage remains on a growth curve (and it will for the next decade, easily), the skills needed to make it work will change as well, and the frenzy for people will continue.

With skills so difficult to come by, the tactics employed in obtaining scarce and desperately needed IT skills are becoming extreme. Among the most common is to simply steal employees from competitors, pre-trained, by offering either better pay or a more attractive working environment. This practice can put the IT shops that provide a lot of training at a disadvantage – in some cases they become deliberate targets. It's a strategic option: to train, or to poach.

The methods employed in the poaching game are as desperate as the skills shortage is extreme. Many organisations have gone well beyond the standard sources of recruiting (head-hunters, job fairs, advertising, sponsoring events) and have begun guerrilla tactics. Extreme methods that have begun to reach "commonplace" status in some highly competitive areas include planting attendees at seemingly unrelated events such as winery festivals, and scooping out the fishbowl of business cards (for a "win-a-free-lunch" draw) in restaurants near competitors. Smart organisations also recognise that it pays to keep a long-term view and a positive relationship. Acknowledging that nothing is forever, most Silicon Valley firms now point with pride to their "re-hire" rates, with many of their employees enjoying a third or fourth pass through the company.

Since successful outsourcing depends heavily on sustaining a cadre of staff and on access to a variety of skills in chronic shortage, many desperate managers (both within outsourced service providers and their customers) grab for the closest available body and end up settling for a modicum of the necessary skill. For an outsourced service provider, there is a definite requirement for people to do a defined job. If they are short of people, they are short of capacity. In these situations, anything at all seems preferable to incapacity. It's a tough trade-off, and may seem "better than nothing". But, in fact, it could well be much worse than nothing.

The top performers in an organisation regularly account for a level of productivity and performance that is an order of magnitude greater than the average. At the same time, the bottom performers are generally performing at a level almost proportionally below the average[69]. The relative cost to an organisation of having "just any" performer versus having someone at the top levels can easily be the difference between a profitable and money-losing line of business. And it very often is. Mediocrity is no longer sustainable.

What does it take to hold on to the best?

There is no single answer to the question of what it takes to keep the best – but there is most certainly a set of predictors and prescriptive actions that can minimise the likelihood of losing high-calibre people.

The short answer – and it is a heavily laden one – is to make sure they have a good boss[70]. The majority of factors that have the greatest influence on an employee's decision to stay or to leave an organisation are under the direct control of that person's immediate manager. Company-wide initiatives such as flextime, profit sharing, casual dress and the like are not without their merits. They make significant contributions to overall organisational culture and also become part of the arsenal that the aforementioned manager is able to call upon. But for a single pressure point, the direct manager is it.

There are many tools and techniques that direct managers can employ. The first is to understand whether and where a potential departure problem exists. There are many known predictors of the probability that a worker will leave a job. Of these, the single best predictor is the articulated desire to leave. Once a worker has come to the point of actually saying he or she is thinking of working elsewhere, they're essentially already gone. Responding to a stated desire to leave is a bit like closing the barn door after the horse is gone: it is necessary to intervene earlier[71].

The participants in the research associated with this book, each of which is described in the case studies in Chapter Four, took part in a survey of the skills and motivators of their key asset – their people – in order to better understand their respective positions regarding skill retention. Selected summary data from that survey is presented here.

People spend most of their waking hours in the work environment. Its components and nature are a huge influence on the attitude of workers. When asked to indicate which of a variety of elements that constitute the work environment were most important to them for job satisfaction, respondents indicated resoundingly that, above all, they want to feel good about what they're doing. Topping the list as most important to job satisfaction was having a sense of achievement, followed closely by having a good balance between work life and personal life. Though respondents want to feel certain that they're being treated fairly as regards remuneration (market rate salary was fifth on the list), salary increase was well down the list, behind career opportunities, teamwork, non-monetary recognition, and access to tools and to experts.

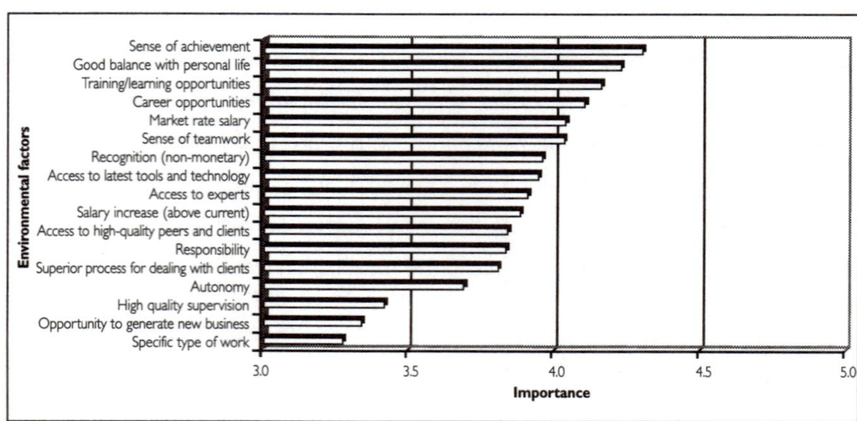

Though all factors rate as at least "important" on average (a score of 3.0 indicates "important" and a score of 5.0 indicates "extremely important"), the exact type of work is least important of all factors. This is a promising finding in an age when constant re-skilling is more and more a necessity – people are adaptable to the specific content of their work (and, in fact, desire a high content of training and learning).

Having assessed the importance of these environmental factors, our analysis demonstrates that their status is quite revealing. Respondents were asked to estimate their own skill levels on a variety of parameters. An inspection of the influence of environmental factors on the highly skilled versus those of average (self-assessed) skill levels indicated virtually no difference in the importance of these factors. Nevertheless, there was a marked difference in the environmental sense between those committed to staying with the organisation and those with a high likelihood of leaving.

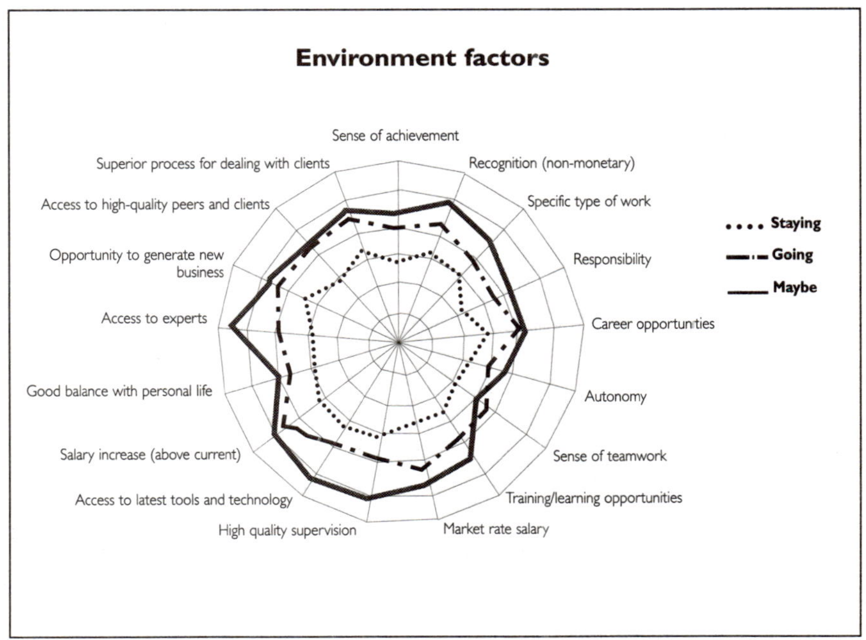

Respondents were asked to indicate their current intentions regarding staying with or leaving their current employers. The full set of possible responses was reduced to three categories: likely to stay; might stay/might go; and likely to leave. The centre of the chart above represents a top assessment of "excellent", with the perimeter representing an assessment of "poor". A tight circle around the bull's eye would be the ideal situation of an "excellent" assessment for all factors. This data indicates that those who are most likely to stay with their current employer have the highest assessment of the current environment. This is as one would expect. What is perhaps more surprising – and something that all managers should note – is that it is not those who have begun to take steps to leave who rate the current environment lowest. The group on the borderline, those who have thought of making a move but have taken no action, gives the lowest rating. Having done nothing specific, these disgruntled individuals will be harder to spot, but they are quite obviously at greatest risk.

The in-demand professional will invariably be offered attractive compensation options to move to another employer. For many technical professionals in the developed world (the profile is different in the developing world), that money ceases to act as a significant motivator fairly quickly. There is a threshold (and it is fairly high in many cases) below which an employer's compensation offer can't go – but offering, say, a doubling of a comfortable salary will come nowhere near to doubling the likelihood of a reluctant employee sticking around. Like hygiene, it's missed when it's not there, but it is not a primary motivator.

What does it take to jeopardise your key assets?

People make the decision to change employers for a wide variety of reasons, but the most prevalent among professionals in this region is that they're bored. With high demand for their skills and compensation requirements reasonably met, the obvious levers are not in play. It is boredom and poor feedback that send people packing. When asked to describe their employment histories, respondents indicated that the greatest influence on their decisions

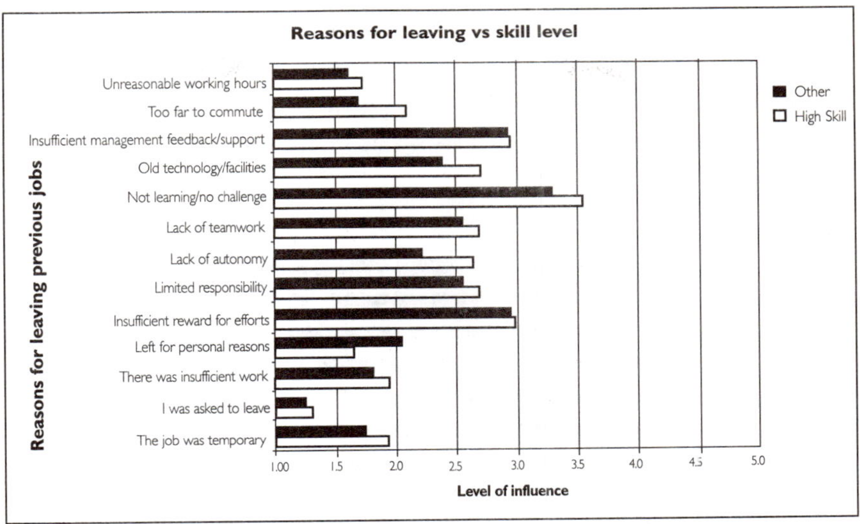

to leave previous jobs was a dearth of learning opportunities and a lack of challenge.

The other factors with a level of influence worth noting (a score of 3.0 indicates "some influence"; a score of 2.0 indicates "little influence") are low levels of management support or feedback and insufficient reward for effort. These factors are ones requiring the much sought direct management attention and hence are often in short supply. This ranking of influencing factors partly explains why the most commonly used management incentive for employee retention is the offer of training or education[72]. This inducement clearly aligns with employee preferences (lack of learning opportunities tops the regret list) and has the added bonus of requiring fairly little direct management intervention. Though there were some differences between them, the patterns are generally the same for employees of high and average self-assessed skill levels.

Armed with the knowledge of what turns employees off, the best organisations also know what attracts and keeps them. The flip side of a paucity of interesting work is the presence of career opportunities and challenge. Respondents found it much easier to indicate a strong degree of influence on changing jobs due to factors related to *the jobs they were going to* rather than the jobs they were leaving. Employers looking to keep good people must have a good understanding of what the best and brightest are being offered. Making people happy is not enough – it is imperative to make them feel certain that there isn't a better offer around the corner.

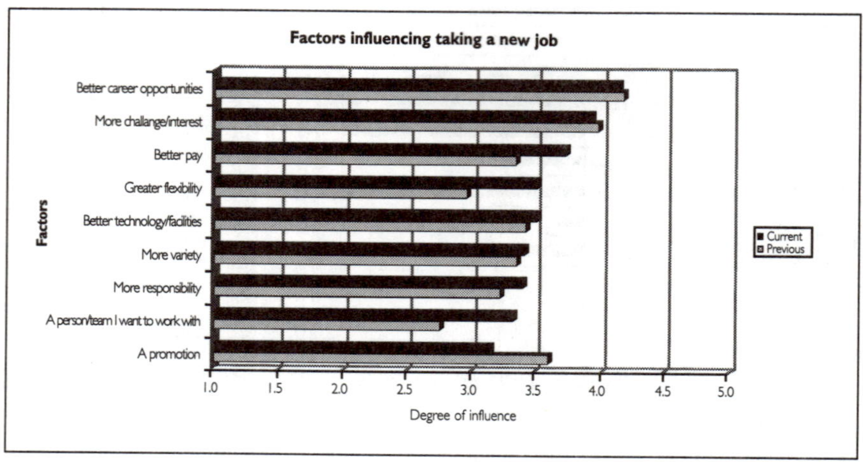

This means a constant monitoring, not only of employees' attitudes, but also of competitors' environments. The best people will get multiple offers on a regular basis. The challenge is to ensure that the environment that they are in offers them what they're being offered elsewhere. It is a big effort and a major upheaval to change jobs. Most people would rather not do it. Employers have that on their side. What is necessary is to understand what would lure employees away – and then offer it to them, without being asked. This is what competitors are doing. If you don't do it first, they will almost certainly co-opt your top guns.

In a fair number of instances, workers are taking jobs with competitors because they're simply too good to pass up. Particularly for younger workers with lower salaries, the differences in compensation can be substantial. In spite of the previous indication that a stated intention to leave was as good as an assurance, it may well be worth the effort to make an equally exorbitant counteroffer. In many instances, the workers don't particularly want to leave the environment – they'd stay with specific modifications to their compensation or conditions. It may be late, but better late than never: the cost of replacement is simply too high to give up without a fight.

In order to intervene early against employee and skill loss, employees' motivators must be understood. It is important to realise that for the vast majority of highly skilled professionals, loyalty is to their team, not to their particular employers. You'll almost never hear a developer or a project manager (even though they may work on financial systems for a large bank) say that they "work for a bank". They will be far more likely to describe themselves in terms of their immediate function or team.

Professional affiliation is a strong factor in retention. Many organisations misunderstand the nature of professional affiliation, however. People feel the greatest commitment to the team with which they work most directly. This means that the employer matters less to employees than it once did. In cases of outsourcing, where there may be co-location, for example, the outsourced staff may feel ambiguous about which legal entity is their "employer" – there's the organisation that signs their pay cheque; and there's the organisation to which they report; and there's the organisation that houses their equipment and desk; and there's the organisation that they originally joined.

The best and the brightest in the field tend to attract each other. The prospect of working with smart people on challenging projects is as much a motivator

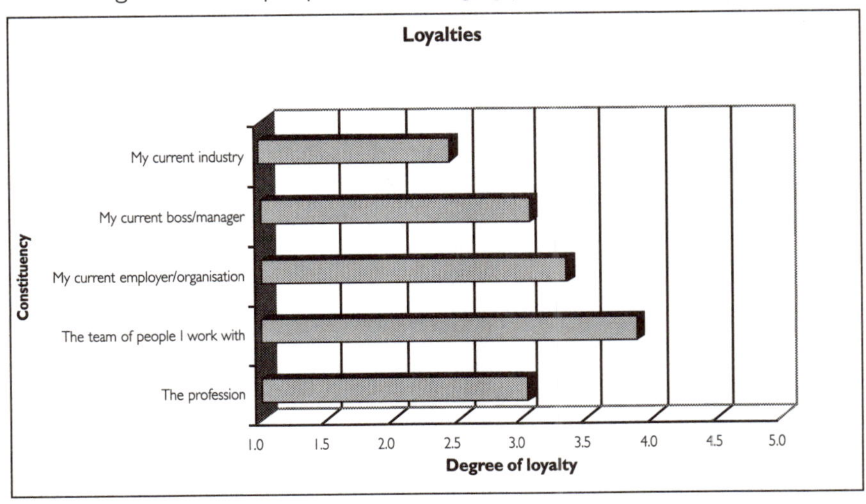

as any for many professionals. The bright ones also like to keep themselves that way and require an environment that allows for constant skill upgrading, retraining, learning and experimentation. Identity, and therefore motivation, comes from that professional association. This strong affiliation will give an edge to firms in which the specialist professional function has a strong reputation. In instances where the core business matches that of the professional, outsourced service providers have a marked advantage.

The work environment plays its part, too. There are a wide variety of possible factors that can influence whether a particular environment is conducive to high morale, productivity and attracting the best people. The sheer number of possible permutations of variables means that there is no single ideal environment. This doesn't mean that anyone is off the hook, however – some factors are clearly important for the majority of people and to allow degradation of those elements in the work environment is management folly.

Risking oversimplification, there is a basic set of rules to follow that will go a long way toward ensuring that the retention of skills is handled in the best possible way in any particular organisation. This checklist is outlined below.

- Catch the problem before the point of no return

It is far more expensive to obtain and train than to retain: pay attention to the factors that will lead people to the door. Anticipate and take pre-emptive action.

- "Spending your way out" is a short-term solution

For the most part, salary increases will have a short-term effect – and it's a strategy that's very easy for competitors to imitate. Compensation can't be ignored, but a focus on the work environment would yield a better return.

- Customise the work environment and incentives

No set of incentives will work for all employees. Understand the ones that will work best for the type of people and skills that are the most difficult to retain. Technical specialists, in general, respond best to short-term monetary incentives, while business technologists and consultants go more for rewards that boost status, career or long-term financial gain.

• Ask them

There are many management approaches for improving the environment and keeping the best people. Knowing which of these will have the greatest impact is tricky. The best advice in trying to choose is: ask. So you don't have to guess.

References

[66]*Harkins, Philip J, "Why Employees Stay - Or Go", Workforce Magazine, October 1998*

[67]*U.S. Department of Labor, Employment and Training Administration, http://www.doleta.gov/h-1b/*

[68]*American Immigration Law Foundation, Immigration Policy Reports, http://www.ailf.org/polrep/*

[69]*Imperato, Gina, "How to Hire the Next Michael Jordan", Fast Company, December, 1998.*

[70]*Kaye, Beverly and Sharon Jordan-Evans, Love 'Em or Lose 'Em, Berrett-Koehler, 1999.*

[71]*Hurley, Margaret, "IT Skill Retention", NNI: Opinion, 4 (3), 1999.*

[72]*Training as a Recruitment Tool, Watson Wyatt, 1999.*

Chapter Six

WHAT DO YOU EXPECT?

The research elucidated in this book and in many other works on the topic of outsourcing is necessarily limited to reviews of current status and of history. For most people grappling with the associated issues on a daily basis, a reasonably accurate view of what to expect in the future would make a major difference in their choices in and their success. If the designers of the early outsourcing arrangements for PC hardware, for example, were able to predict the extent and duration of the price/performance profile of PCs, they would very likely have come up with different arrangements than they did. Arrangements for PC hardware provision that were applauded in the early days turned into big losers for the buyers within a year or two: what started out as a "hard bargain" fast disintegrated into a sucker's deal.

With those lessons in mind, the research group here attempts some predictions – that is, foretelling based on observation and experience – about what buyers and vendors can expect as significant influences on the practice of alternative sourcing in business.

What to expect from the environment

Macro-level environmental factors will have major effects on the style and practice of outsourcing as it continues to evolve. These factors, which are already impinging on every aspect of economic, political, commercial and social life, are beyond the control of individual organisations or in most cases even governments, but, as always, firms will distinguish themselves for good or ill in how they respond to these forces.

Globalisation

Virtually any service with a mainly intellectual (as opposed to physical presence) requirement is feasibly performed at a distance from the service's recipient. Writing, research, instruction, direction, help, design, programming, creation, refinement, editing, monitoring, tabulating and reviewing are but a few of the things that can be (and regularly are) done at a distance and even asynchronously. If a service can be performed at a separate location than that of the recipient of the service, then it can theoretically be performed anywhere: service providers could come from anywhere around the globe.

The advent of widespread and reliable telecommunications has made this theoretical possibility a reality.

One of the clearest cases in point is the widespread use of computer programming expertise based in India. Long-standing programs in India that have emphasised computer science education have resulted in a rich source of much-needed technical skill in India. There are now many North American- and European-based computer systems development projects that are being manned from India. Requirements and specifications are sent to the technical team in India, where the work is executed. This arrangement includes not only an economic advantage (personnel costs are still much lower in India than in many other countries) but also a time zone advantage: a significant amount of project work is completed while the customer sleeps and is available the next morning.

There are many other permutations of this model. Concerted efforts to develop specific skill sets are increasingly part of government policy in a variety of developing countries. Programming and call centres are currently the most prevalent areas of "off-shore" sourcing work, but few service areas are exempt, ultimately.

The implications of this phenomenon are that both buyers and sellers of services must keep keenly aware of seemingly irrelevant developments. At a macro level, such things as the availability of wireless Internet service in remote villages in Pakistan or the demand for fashion accessories among teenagers in Japan could have a real and lasting impact on a service offering that was assumed would always be local. At a lower level, an awareness of the more immediate needs in the environment – for example, the expansion of a partner's or competitor's service line to include 24-hour coverage or to include support in Spanish and Chinese – is essential to understanding the viability of continued local service provision. This awareness is also essential to anticipating and developing the skill sets that will be in most urgent demand in the short term.

Regionalisation

The case of India's emphasis on computer technical skills illustrates the strength of regions as well as globalisation. While the Indian concept of concerted skill development is theoretically easy to copy, many have attempted it and failed. Others have succeeded in a less dramatic fashion: Russia and Ireland are rich sources of offshore programming resource, for example. What the Indian example illustrates is the sustainability of strengths in a region, a sustainability resulting from the environment and history. The strength could come from several sources: government initiatives (the development of semiconductors in Japan is the classic example); the education system; natural resources; geographic placement; and language history are some of the major ones. Regions have patterns of economic development and innovation that have an impact on their ability to compete. For Australian companies and others in the Pacific Rim, it is essential to recognise the regional strengths and weaknesses and use them. The big mistake that many organisations (especially those expanding internationally) make is to ignore regional differences and history.

For example, many non-US-based wireless vendors spent a great deal of time and effort trying to sell a superior technology – GSM phones – in the US, a region known as an early adopter of such personal technologies. Though the changeover will happen eventually, it will be at a much slower pace than these vendors assumed. They made the mistake of ignoring the regional history, one rooted in the early North American adoption of a different infrastructure that doesn't support GSM and that is not going away quietly. The assumption that the region would avidly adopt new technology was correct, but that was insufficient for success. The underpinnings of the region have to be considered or the picture is incomplete.

Skill infrastructures emerge in much the same way, usually precipitating or following and feeding a major industry. Many emerging worldwide skill requirements are based on technologies and services that originated (in the case of electronic commerce, for example) in Silicon Valley. There are a few basic implications for the Pacific Rim in the case of this emerging industry. The first is that, even though there is dispersion in the skill base, the centre of the industry is still heavily weighted toward that region (Silicon Valley) and so it will continue to attract a great proportion of the financial and intellectual capital that the industry requires. Another is that, as the centre of activity, the Silicon Valley region will generally be the starting point and the test bed for many of the associated technologies and techniques. What that means for the Pacific region is that it will continue to be unlikely that it will have to deal with version 1.0 of many of these service offerings. The Pacific Rim will adopt many of these offerings after they've had a chance to mature a bit elsewhere. Some of the methodological kinks will have been worked out, minimising some of the risk, but labour sourcing and training will be a problem for some time and the services may be expensive or less than reliable in terms of support availability.

Other areas of the Pacific Rim, however, will "leapfrog" technologies. Developing countries in the region do not have the entrenched infrastructure associated with technology deployment that the region's developed countries do. China, for example, will circumvent the establishment of landline phones over most of its territory and go straight for wide dissemination of wireless technology. The implications of a massive, entirely new, customer base for a technology in its early stages are significant. This user base will have a profound impact on the direction of wireless technologies. This user base is one that uses a non-Roman text and that has much lower literacy levels than the established user base for these technologies. The effects of such factors will be significant: obvious fallout from the mobile-phones-in-China scenario, for example, will be increased demand for user interface development skills and Chinese language support. Which countries and organisations in the region are best positioned to take advantage of these developments? Without doubt, they are the ones that have already recognised the trend.

Low-hanging fruit, change and innovation

As the practice of outsourcing becomes more commonplace, an increasing number of outsourced service offerings are approaching the "mature" end of the life cycle curve. Many would conclude from this that the low-hanging fruit of profitable offerings and strategic realignment has been plucked and the outsourcing trend has seen its day. The margins attainable by vendors in the early days of an offering may not be repeatable, but the early days of an offering are also notoriously low in capacity. That's the thing about low-hanging fruit: like innovation, there generally isn't a lot of it to be had. None of this means that the profit has been kicked out of the equation. It does reinforce the requirement for continuous innovation, though.

All of the varying versions of the life cycle model depicted in Chapter Two agree that fundamental changes are to be expected at different points in the life cycle. One of the main characteristics of a product or service that has reached maturity is that it experiences fairly little change in its composition after that point – unless its fundamental form is changed. This requires a change in one of its basic components: the underlying technology, the method of sales and remuneration, the method of delivery or the business processes surrounding it.

In many ways, the ability to revert to the environment that fostered the innovation that established the product or service requires a scaling back: size is an influence. Although most patents and product development is owned and executed by large organisations, most good ideas originally come out of small places[73]. Small groups of people are the most likely source of innovations. Large organisations either tend to buy them after they've been developed or they work very hard to nurture that small-group, start-up feel within the larger firm. There's a reason, after all, that (successful) R&D environments are so quirky and removed from the centre of the business. Large organisations that succeed in breathing new life into mature offerings usually do so by spinning off subsets of the groups that are looking after the mature product.[74]

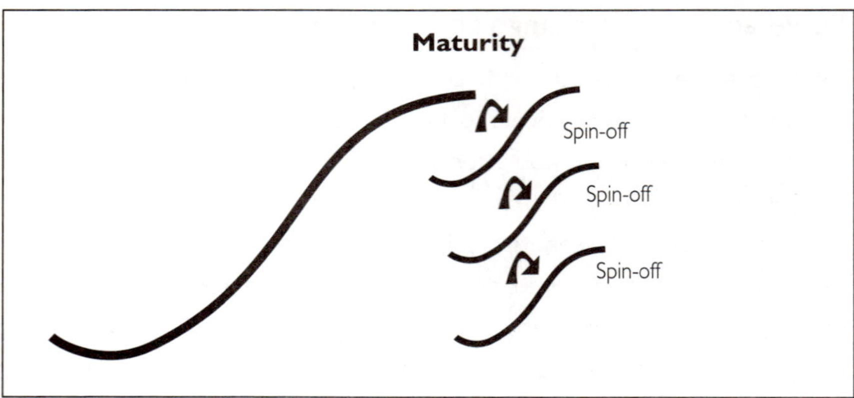

Technology has had a lot of attention as the conduit for innovation, and with good reason. Advances in technologies – and not just information technologies, although these are the most evident to most observers – are seen as the harbinger of still further technological advances. A lot of faith and attention are given to technologies as stand-alone phenomena that will allow further growth, productivity, change and advancement. But technological advances are only as good as the uses that are made of them, the processes around them. Technologies and processes must grow in tandem, and in fact, there is much evidence to suggest that they do.

A recent Australian study[75] showed that innovation levels varied by industry and by company size. Overall, the level of non-technological innovation (including such things as process and product innovation) was greater than the level of technological innovation.

Percent of organisations indicating technological innovation	Percent of organisations indicating non-technological innovation
12.2%	13.8%

These statistics suggest that much of the benefit of the unique differentiators that result from the innovation of knowledge workers happens independently of technology. Technology is a tremendous catalyst, but it is not the core. Its usefulness is as a supplement and an enhancement of workers' activities. Far too often, work is defined in the reverse: as the ability to employ technology.

Workers – and particularly those whose productivity is most under scrutiny in the New Economy, knowledge workers – should not work on their computers: their computers should work for them.

The potential and the capability of technology are getting a lot of attention, and rightly so. Technology is doing tremendous things. When technology (which is the "how") precedes a clear definition of the end result (the "what"), some inappropriate activities often result. A scan of most organisations would demonstrate that there is still a significant mismatch between what people are doing and what they were hired for – and much of that mismatch is a result of technologies that create as much effort as they save.

Recent research indicates that the pursuit of a 1:1 ratio of workstations to users and the successful implementation of standard PC-based office tools across the corporate world has resulted in a misalignment of skills. It appears that our most highly paid and uniquely skilled resources are spending disproportionate amounts of time operating basic PC tools[76].

Whether or not it is the right path to the desired result, the philosophy around downsizing is that organisations should be able to do more with less. In areas where the objective is greater volume of physical throughput, that is actually being accomplished: the manufacturing sector has achieved incredible increases in productivity. But, where the rest of us are concerned (and this includes the administrative functions of manufacturing organisations), the picture is a bit less bright. In the areas where most outsourcing is being done – the white-collar realm – the productivity achieved through the application of technology is far less impressive. Rather than applying our knowledge, we're using the benefits afforded by innovation and technology (more time) to do the clerical tasks of a reduced headcount. Technology only replaced a portion of the administrative and clerical jobs that were eliminated: the other parts of those jobs went to the financial analysts and engineers and biologists and economists. The greatest challenge in the future of outsourcing will be recognising and achieving these elusive technology benefits and ensuring, in a demonstrable fashion, that these key professionals are actually free to spend the majority of their time doing the jobs for which they were hired.

The blurring boundary of the organisation

Technology advances are not achieved in a significant way unless and until corresponding changes occur in the surrounding processes and organisations. In advancing to the Industrial Era, this meant the break-up of small cottage industries as the dominant organisational form for manufacturing and, eventually, even of the family farm as the concomitant mode of agricultural organisation. In the New Economy, this means the break-up of the hierarchical organisation form that was developed in the Industrial Era. (This argument is explored more completely in Chapter Two.)

Several researchers and experts share this view. "Firms in the network era consist of the cooperation of a number of legally independent corporations held together by central orchestration and rational coordination. This development redefines the concept of the firm as an entity: it is no longer clearly defined, incorporated or clearly owned.[77]"

There is much evidence that this is more and more the case. Changes to organisational boundaries are evidenced by the number of independent contractors, by the number of employers that individuals have over their working lives and by the multiple identities that people carry in their professional lives. In the New Economy, it is very common for many previously unrelated identities to overlap: the professors are also the investors and the investors are the inventors and the inventors are the managers. These people may work within an organisation in a traditional mode. They may also *at the same time* advise another organisation. They may teach people that work in a competing organisation. Where do they really work? What is their organisation?

This phenomenon blurs the edges of what had previously been easy to see as the clearly demarcated organisation. Adding further to this blurring is the prominent presence of outsourcing. One organisation pays the employees, but service is to another. In providing the service, employees do so under the policies and procedures of one organisation, while interacting with and serving the needs of another entity.

These factors all work together to demonstrate that the organisational forms with which we are most familiar are beginning to break down and are accommodating "outsiders" in a fairly fluid and efficient manner. The boundaries of the organisation are beginning to blur and the definition of something new is emerging.

The combination of changing identities, new innovation, global access, new skill requirements and new organisational forms are working to redefine the jobs that people do. There are many jobs for which the descriptions have not yet been written, jobs that will come to wield tremendous power and influence and for which demand will be very high over the next decade. The importance of a Webmaster could not even have been imagined ten years ago. The same sort of changes will continue, and outsourcing will be an essential element in placing these key skills where they are needed.

Top 10 New Most Powerful People by 2005

- Chief Monitoring Officer
- E-marketplace Officer
- Marketing Executives
- E-Deal Makers
- CRM Analytic Experts
- Transaction "Cops"
- HR Exectives
- E-Business Integrators
- Economists
- Anthropologists

Gartner Group, 2000

Positions specifically related to outsourcing will emerge. In addition to the Steward role (see Chapter Two), there will emerge a position at the executive level that will be responsible for the management of the full range of available resources. This Chief Resource Officer[78] will monitor the various sources of skill and technology and the relationships among them.

With organisational boundaries blurring, jobs changing significantly and loyalties shifting (see Chapter Five), it is increasingly important for organisations to monitor, manage and maintain the intellectual assets necessary to run the business.

For an increasing number of organisations, the most meaningful measure of assets is based on intellectual capital as much as physical capital. Intellectual capital consists of three major components: knowledge capital, structural capital and relationship capital. Knowledge capital and relationship capital reside in large measure in the minds and actions of people.

For any manager, the concept of capital investment is a basic one: for any such investment, a calculable return is expected. The model with which most of us are familiar and with which must of us have been educated assumes that capital is physical, or is easily translated to the physical. Much of it is, of course. But business invests no less in intellectual capital.

Intellectual capital is comprised – together with supporting infrastructure and existing relationships with customers – of human capital: the workers in and around the organisation. We build intellectual capital by investing in infrastructure to build organisational capability. Offices, computer networks, organisational structures and corporate visions are all part of the infrastructure of intellectual capital. We further build intellectual capital by investing in customer relationships. Customer loyalty programs are a case in point, with goodwill the traditional expected return. Finally, we invest in building the human capital – the knowledge, skills and loyalty of those associated with an organisation.

What is it about the knowledge worker that's different from the way of working we've assumed before? It's simply this: while the other pieces of intellectual capital do things, knowledge workers *know* things. It's not just an enhanced ability to do things that organisations are striving for now. It's an enhanced ability to know how to dynamically, creatively and profitably put all the pieces of capital together to create an output.

This knowledge is what binds the elements of intellectual capital together. The three pieces are inextricably intertwined – if you lose one piece, some of the others may go along with it. For example, people leaving a firm will often take some of the customer capital along with them; or the loss of their knowledge will devalue the operating effectiveness of the infrastructure.

Many business performance measures beyond cost and revenue are being given tremendous lip service: even the most business-ignorant technician knows to recite that a given technology product will "provide your company with competitive advantage". The beauty of a pitch like this is that the concept of what truly constitutes competitive advantage is ill understood. Without knowing what it really means, achievement or non-achievement is difficult to prove or refute.

The starting point, then, is understanding what competitive advantage really is today. The specifics vary by industry and objectives, but in any case it is something that is 1) unique, 2) lasting and 3) puts you at the forefront[79]. Think for a moment about these three criteria. No product, idea or technology can, on its own, meet all three. In the words of a senior manager in a leading Canadian organisation, "The only true competitive advantage lies in the hearts and minds of the people who work in and around your organisation[80]."

It isn't enough, however, to recognise that the knowledge worker is essential to success. Disparate views from a collection of knowledgeable, creative individuals will still be disparate views. The cadre of knowledge workers that a forward-thinking organisation invests in must be working toward a common goal. This is something greater than a vision or mission statement: even the best of these will be interpreted in a variety of ways by a variety of people. Each views the desired end result through a different lens.

Moving from a set of individual (and different) mindsets to a collective mindset is a necessary step toward realising the full potential of the intellectual capital of the organisation: getting individuals and teams to work toward a singular, focused goal that is explicitly understood by all to be the same thing. Many organisations think they've achieved this, pointing to proclamations emblazoned on the walls of every office. Simply perceiving the words is insufficient. A common knowledge of the true intention of those words is required. The words should not only be recognised, but should be translated in a consistent fashion across the organisation. This becomes a sort of breaking down of the messages into the components that will be understood by all, regardless of the lens through which they are viewed.

Achievement of true common vision is a challenge, and an even greater one when the perspectives are still more diverse, by virtue of a variety of organisational positions. In an outsourcing arrangement, there are multiple visions to be understood – those of the supplier and those of the buyer – and there are multiple perspectives within each organisation. The challenge is greater, and the need to meet the challenge greater still. The possible advantage that an outsourcing arrangement has is that there is a requirement for all concerned parties to explicitly discuss objectives and the metrics via which all will agree that they have been met. This exercise may serve to give all parties a common understanding. Though often done as a legal and contractual obligation, it is absolutely crucial in this regard.

References

[73]*Hurley, Margaret, "True global trading": reaching the other 90% of the world, chapter in Changing Business directions for the 21st Century, Addison Wesley, Amsterdam, 200*

[74]*Adizes, Ichak, Corporate Life cycles, Prentice Hall, 1988, with input from Gerry Faust, PhD*

[75]*"Innovation in Industry", Australian Bureau of Statistics Information Paper, Catalogue No. 8117.0, Canberra, 1995*

[76]*Gibbs, W. Wayt, "Taking Computers to Task", Scientific American, 277 (1) July 1997*

[77]*Damen, Ger, Han van der Zee and Hans Strikwerda, "Introduction: Business Designs for the 21st Century", chapter in Changing Business Designs for the 21st Century, Addison Wesley, Amsterdam, 2000.*

[78]*Quinn, James Brian, "Managing Outsourcing and Intellect", in conversation with The Outsourcing Institute, http://www.outsourcing.com/buyersite/articles*

[79]*Hurley, Margaret, "Supporting the Knowledge Worker", NNI: Opinion, 2 (3) 1996.*

[80]*Leighton, Helen, Partner in Caravan Consulting, quoted in conversation with the author, February, 2001.*

Chapter Seven

RECOMMENDATIONS

To ensure outsourcing success, companies need to look beyond simple recipes such as tightly written contracts or outsourcing only commodity functions. The cases in Chapter Four simultaneously reinforce the uniqueness of each outsourcing arrangement and highlight the common issues. Many problems can be avoided through learning from the experiences of others. These lessons, the common themes and their interrelations are discussed in this chapter.

One common desire among those participating in the research was to understand how to maximise the likelihood of success in outsourcing. Motives for outsourcing cannot always be determined by a unique, tangible criterion. Consequently, the level of success is not precisely measurable in an objective sense. Moreover, success or failure can be contingent on a myriad of factors, including ones quite distinct from the outsourcing arrangement itself. Our cases show that service quality provided by the vendor and partnership elements such as trust, cooperation and communication affect the overall success of the outsourcing arrangement. These findings are reinforced in other research[81].

Based on lessons learned from the cases, surveys and other group research, major findings and recommendations are presented here. Some of the lessons are applicable to any participant in an outsourcing arrangement. Others have most resonance with vendors of outsourced services, still others with buyers. All are important in ensuring fruitful outsourcing agreements.

Lessons for all of us

The case studies and the reviews of economic trends and management frameworks have demonstrated the key roles that innovation and reinvention have played and will continue to play in doing business successfully. Part of that necessity is the need for focus and specialisation: the precise opposites of the 19th- and 20th-century business ideal of vertical integration. The pace of change and growth, the dramatic transformations, leaps and spin-offs required in the current environment (as described in Chapters Two and Four) mean that no organisation can do it all. Large organisations lack the agility; small organisations lack the infrastructure. Cooperation, interaction, alliance, partnership, mutual assistance and risk sharing are all necessary for current-day business. There is interdependence among businesses now that has never existed on this scale, at this magnitude.

What this means is that the nature and terms around many organisational interactions are not intuitive, are not a matter of standard business procedure. Though developing, many of the forms of agreement are still being tried and tested. Outsourcing is one categorisation of a range of potential interactions among organisations. It is, in many instances, mature – particularly in arrangements that relate to physical jobs or materials. In these areas, the prime and peripheral parties all have a reasonable experiential base of expectations. But in the emerging areas of service- and intellect-based offerings, the business standards are less developed. Not only the primary parties (the ostensible buyer and seller), but also a range of tertiary parties, must develop their roles and positions.

Contract and copyright law, for example, are relatively easy to apply in a range of service provision options. But their basic assumptions of buyer and seller, of where the benefit lies in a transaction, are under challenge. This means that the roles of such parties as lawyers, advisors, consultants – and even customers and suppliers – are simultaneously crucial and questionable. In changing circumstances, it is necessary to keep up to date, remain innovative and stay ahead of the competition. Third parties can be the best means of achieving this. They can also be dangerously mired in the standards and assumptions of the past, and become a detriment to advancement.

End customers (i.e., the customer's customer – the recipient of outsourced call centre support or the recipient of the outsourced fulfilment service) will have a much more direct voice in the development of future arrangements. Most existing outsourcing agreements are struck between two entities, each making its own assumptions about the impact of the agreement on other parties. Companies are emphasising a core competency focus, the New Economy necessitates impromptu alliances, global economic forces result in wholesale organisational and industry transformation, and the communication modes established by the Internet have become common business practice. This means that inter-company agreements will certainly expand and change to include a wide variety of contributors. These contributors will be involved in increasingly detailed and structured ways, ultimately becoming integral parts of agreements and ultimately of the organisational form itself. The currently dominant forms of outsourcing will continue to exist, but many other permutations will emerge to augment these arrangements and to fit with and exploit economic realities. Outsourcing is dead – long live outsourcing!

The current form of agreement will remain attractive, perhaps well beyond its usefulness, in part because it has the most well defined approach to making money and achieving benefit. The table below depicts a few of the variants that are easily foreseeable given current business conditions.

✔ = current role (P) = potential role

	Objectives	Terms	Performance Monitoring	Payment
Outsourcing "buyer"	✔	✔	✔	✔
Outsourced service provider	✔	✔	✔	✔
Customer of buyer	(P)	(P)	(P)	(P)
Customer of customer	(P)	(P)	(P)	(P)
Supplier of customer	(P)	(P)	(P)	(P)
Supplier of outsourcer	(P)	(P)	(P)	(P)
Partner of buyer	(P)	(P)	(P)	(P)
Auditor		(P)	(P)	
Business advisor	(P)	(P)	(P)	
Legal/structural advisor	(P)	(P)		

Increased involvement from multiple parties will continue to redefine the edges of the organisation and the nature of sourcing arrangements. Leading business experts cite this in predicting the demise of conventional outsourcing: "Managers will no longer view the integrated corporation as the starting point for assigning tasks and functions. Rather, they will begin with a customer value proposition and a blank slate for the production and delivery infrastructure."[82] We all have a role to play in the development of outsourcing and the reshaping of the organisational forms that will propel business forward in the New Economy. Whether we recognise that role at the right time and play it properly will define the difference between sustainability and dissolution.

Regardless of role, certain lessons and strategies are useful to any player in the outsourcing game. Our overview of life cycle phenomena and the in-depth view of the reasons behind outsourcing decisions enable us to see a general pattern that is useful to buyer and supplier, to neophyte and veteran. An ability to categorise the decisions and reasons, to recognise how and why decisions are being made and to assess the fit of offerings to need – these are the essential ingredients for identifying and developing the correct strategic approach to outsourcing.

Life cycle maturity	Cost	Skill
Mature	Least-cost approach Conventional contract	Pick and choose Add-on agreement
Early stage	Fluid arrangement Short contracts	Establish mind share Partnerships

Reasons for outsourcing

There has been much emphasis on the superiority of certain styles of sourcing arrangement – partnerships over conventional contracting arrangements, for example. The idea that a form is superior in and of itself is misleading. A form of organisation and a strategy for sourcing is appropriate for a given circumstance. Recognising the contributing factors that determine what is appropriate is the real management skill. That is no easy task. There is strong opinion in the marketplace that "you actually need a higher quality of management in order to outsource successfully.[83]" An ability to assess the situation and apply the right approach, with the right partners, is the scarce skill set. With the background of life cycle frameworks (Chapter Two) and outsourcing drivers (Chapter Four) as a grounding, the fundamental recommendations for strategies to pursue in key situations are given above. They are basic necessities of the skilled outsourcing manager's toolkit.

Recommendations for buyers

Outsourcing is redefining business. Outsourcing allows organisations to focus on their core competencies and create networks of outside expert suppliers for critical – but non-core – support skills. These organisations bring together the best talents of multiple firms and are rapidly replacing traditional, vertically integrated, self-sufficient organisations.

In the abstract, the reasons for outsourcing are compelling. In many instances, the pressures to outsource are very forceful. For those under these pressures, a key set of recommendations has emerged from the research:

- Do it for the right reasons
- Do it when the time is right
- Choose the right supplier
- Design the agreement well
- Actively manage the contract
- Look after people

Do it for the right reasons

Far too often, the impetus for outsourcing is unrelated to the things that outsourcing can actually achieve. Though it is often the unspoken driver, "achieving political ends" will never make the list of outsourcing accomplishments. The strategies and successes outlined in the case studies illustrate the conditions and drivers that are likely to meet with success. An organisation considering outsourcing must first identify its strategic reasons for outsourcing and establish clear expectations of why this is being done and a clear understanding of what is to be achieved. An important success factor is the buyer's ability to base its decision on clear, attainable goals. With all successful cases, there is a clear connection between motives and business decisions[84]. The bottom line is: make sure outsourcing is done for the right reasons. This is important because it assists in determining the most appropriate outsourcing model (see Chapter Three) that should be used to fulfil goals. Furthermore, the strategic reasoning behind the decision to outsource also helps in identifying an appropriate vendor whose way of operating is closely aligned with the buyer's objectives.

Too often organisations get excited about outsourcing because it represents a chance to offload a problem they haven't been able to solve themselves. Outsourcing needs to be justified on different criteria. When a sourcing strategy is pursued for the wrong reasons the user ends up paying through the nose for other people to manage a mess. The outcome of such a scenario is an instant outsourcing horror story.

Do it when the time is right

In addition to having fully justified intent and appropriate support for outsourcing, an organisation contemplating outsourcing must be organisationally and culturally ready.

How does an organisation know if it's ready? First, support from key stakeholders is crucial. Even more important than mere support is gaining involvement from key stakeholders during the outsourcing evaluation. Research shows that successful outsourcing decisions require a mix of political power and technical skills[85]. Political power helps to enforce the larger business perspective, such as the need for organisation-wide cost reductions, as well as the strength to implement such business initiatives. Technical expertise in particular functional areas provide insight into performance measures, appropriate service levels, price/performance improvements and a host of other issues.

Look at all stakeholders and understand also their placement on the organisational learning curves (Chapter Two). When there is a misalignment in maturity levels among key parties, organisational readiness is questionable.

Choose the right supplier

Though resoundingly obvious, this recommendation is sufficiently ignored that it bears repeating. The crucial point in selecting the 'right' outsourcer is determining which criteria are of uppermost importance to a buyer's organisation. Appropriate selection depends on specific needs and business requirements. The research in this book points out that some companies choose their suppliers according to expertise and cultural fit, whereas others wanted a supplier that has a level of proficiency across a range of competencies and the ability to access global resources.

Equally revealing are some cases of outsourcing failure. Some outsourcing arrangements have failed because companies did not adequately assess the breadth of a supplier's capabilities, especially its ability to cope with new technology. Entering into a formal outsourcing arrangement with a supplier that cannot deliver the anticipated benefits can lock the user organisation into a deteriorating relationship for several years, limiting the user's ability to achieve its intended business potential.

Defining and finding the 'right' supplier is a difficult task requiring, in some cases, several months of due diligence. The definition of the right supplier is different for each organisation. Essentially, the supplier must have the ability to deliver the outsourcing benefits the buyer expects against the criteria the buyer has set. Buyers must clearly state these if they want to be in a reasonable position to approach the market and find a suitable supplier. The broad criteria that require consideration include the supplier's expertise, capability, values, financial stability, structure and ownership. Both short- and long-term requirements against these criteria are essential.

Once the criteria are established, comparison to the best possible potential suppliers is necessary. Generic supplier information is often available from specific directories to which suppliers contribute. Additional sources of information include:

- The Internet: almost all suppliers advertise their services on the Internet (you may be sceptical about those that don't – particularly IT suppliers). This source is a good starting point in searching for suppliers and establishing their capabilities. Sites such as http://outsourcing.com.au and http://outsourcingcenter.com may be useful starting points.
- Consultants and legal experts: many of the global consultancies and law firms have advisory practices that specialise in outsourcing.

All successful cases in this research used legal experts (e.g., for negotiating contractual details) and some consulted with technical experts or advisors (e.g., for evaluating SLAs). Williamson writes: "It's unrealistic to expect that a company with no prior experience in outsourcing can understand all the implications of a five- or ten-year contract at the beginning".[66] Of those that used advisors, the common feeling was that they were useful during contract negotiations because they had a service level catalogue detailing information on SLAs. The users that contracted the expertise of advisers felt that it placed them in a better position when negotiating the fine details with the service provider. Consultants may also be useful in matching the cultural fit since they possess extensive industry knowledge.

Design the agreement well

The foundation of the relationship between the buyer and supplier in an outsourcing deal is the contract. It outlines the agreed position on a range of commercial points and exposure to various risks of the outsourcing deal, both in terms of what is included and what is excluded from the contractual terms. Given this, buyers should insist on clearly defined, detailed and comprehensive contracts. To achieve this, the buying organisation must establish clear expectations and have the ability to articulate its goals through measurable SLAs. This assists in evaluating the success of the arrangement during various points of the relationship. Organisations may also benefit from the use of external consultants and legal expertise to help define the contract.

There is no denying that contract negotiation is a difficult, time-consuming, yet crucial process. What will keep the team on track is clarity about its outsourcing objectives. All of the effort that has gone into the outsourcing process up to this point will be wasted if the team does not ensure that its requirements are set out with absolute clarity in the contract. An outsourcing contract usually involves both the transfer of assets from the buyer to the supplier and the acquisition of services by the buyer from the supplier. Given this, a typical outsourcing contract comprises four main sections, as follows:[87]

- *Transfers:* This deals with the transfer to the supplier of all 'in-scope' assets, including hardware, software licences, contracts, buildings and personnel.
- *Service provisions:* This section describes the services that the buyer will purchase from the supplier, the scope of the services and performance standards. The detailed service descriptions are usually set out in the SLA, which will be a schedule to the main contract. The SLA will set out specific, quantitative performance obligations, but the contract should also contain general, qualitative standards.
- *General legal provisions:* This section includes details of warranties, indemnities, liability, pricing terms, confidentiality, force majeure, dispute resolution, data protection and termination. Failure to give special consideration to these points can expose the buyer to significant risks.
- *Exit arrangements:* This section describes the rights and liabilities of both parties if a termination arises. This is a high-risk area for the buyer, but planning ahead for two provisions can reduce a number of risks: exit management plan and rights to assets .

Practitioners recommend that during contract development the legal aspects of the contract be broken into two components, the clause and the intent. The clause should encapsulate descriptions of requirements, relevant penalties, strategies for risk mitigations, etc., whereas the intent should answer the following questions: What do we want to achieve? How can we do this?

In addition, two of the most important parts of the contract and the most difficult challenges in negotiating an outsourcing deal are pricing and the SLAs. Clarity and predictability of charges are as important as their absolute level. The pricing mechanism is closely linked to the bonus and penalties regime. These regimes are difficult to get right and both parties need to consider many issues prior to implementing them. A poorly thought-out bonus and/or penalty regime may motivate the vendor to behave in a manner contradictory to the buyer's service objectives.

If the contract is the cornerstone of an outsourcing arrangement, then the SLA is its main structural beam. The SLA describes all of the services the buyer is purchasing, the measures used to monitor the service delivery and the target performance levels. A strong SLA defines clearly what the service delivers, when it delivers it and where it delivers it. It should not enter into a description of how the service is delivered. During the life of the contract the SLA, which evolves to cater for changes to the service portfolio, is a mechanism the buyer can use to retain a degree of control over the service. Often, however, buyers enter outsourcing agreements with less than adequate, or a total absence of, SLAs, thereby opening their organisations to unnecessarily high levels of risk as a result of weak service control. The time and resources required to prepare strong SLAs often deter buyers from preparing SLAs or force them to restrict the effort, resulting in less than adequate agreements. This translates into a weak deal in which the buyer relinquishes ownership of critical services without ensuring that a control mechanism is in place.

Failure to produce SLAs means there is no agreement about the services that the supplier will provide or the metric that will be used to measure performance objectives for the various services. Fortunately (or unfortunately, depending on your perspective) the contract is not kept in the top drawer. Users have become more sophisticated and demanding. Users possess the knowledge, which is formalised in the SLA, to point out the responsibility of the supplier to deliver the service or the project. In addition, some clients prefer the vendor to be proactive and stay abreast of their responsibilities, but this just reinforces that the client cannot outsource the management of the contract.

Actively manage the contract

The most important recommendation for clients is that it is not possible to outsource the responsibility and accountability for achieving goals. One can delegate authority but not responsibility. In all the successful cases outlined here, a dedicated resource was responsible for the arrangement. That person meets regularly with the service provider. Success depends on the client taking ownership and having a sense of control over the client/vendor relationship. This makes sense since both parties have a vested interest in making the arrangement work.

The importance of keeping an in-house management team to oversee the outsourcing project is crucial in monitoring the arrangement. Some users may want to learn more about the activities outsourced in order to understand whether they are getting value for money.

It is common for the outsourcing team to feel as though the deal is over once the contract is signed, but that's just the beginning. This doesn't mean that the milestone shouldn't be celebrated. The most important challenge still lies ahead: to ensure that the deal is effectively managed to deliver outcomes and minimise risk of failure. In order to extract maximum benefit from the outsourcing deal, the buyer must manage its relationship with the supplier in a structured and coordinated manner. This involves managing day-to-day operational activities, monitoring performance, modifying services and assessing the progress of the deal.

Outsourcing contract management is a relatively new requirement in organisations and has resulted in the establishment of new roles. The stewardship model (Chapter Two) is driven mainly by a single executive on the user side, but is best established as a team. The specific composition of the team can vary based on the size of the organisation, complexity of the arrangement, nature of the contract and existing organisational structures on the user side. However, the vendor must also enter the picture at this point.

Regardless of the type of relationship, the supplier must always become a member of the team. Suppliers will not only structurally and continuously receive information on their own performance, methods to improve this performance and insight into the satisfaction level of the user, but they can also actively participate in discussions concerning business requirements and the business impact of and on services to be delivered.

The changing role of senior managers, in the context of outsourcing, has received little attention. The increasing trend toward outsourcing has resulted in a shift from managing an internal department to managing a resource or external vendor. It can be described as an overall shift from a technology focus to a focus on strategic business integration. The implication for managers is that the shift towards outsourcing results in a change of roles – that is, a move from running internal functions to monitoring and evaluating the outsourced function. This requires a multi-skilled manager who primarily seeks to maintain "strategic partnerships". The supplier may help customers create an environment of success, but the ultimate responsibility lies with the customer.

In some organisations, this has meant the establishment of an executive-level position (sometimes known as the Chief Resource Officer) with responsibility for managing outsourcing at a strategic level. "Someone to make sure the supplier is not in conflict with you, for example, to monitor whether they are supplying major competitors, or that they are sufficiently bound to you in the design world so your designs don't sneak out the door. You have to have methodologies and management capability to make sure the supplier is going to work on your behalf at all times. This takes a different set of skills."[88]

With these new changes comes the demand for a new skill set. Users need to determine whether or not they have these skills in-house. This involves forward thinking and planning to either retrain or recruit people that have the ability to manage the contract properly. Other crucial skills include: coordinating user demand and supplier supply, resolving conflicts, understanding the contract's contents, monitoring supplier performance and applying penalties as a last resort.

Client organisations approaching the end of their contracts are faced with the inevitable question: do we renew the contract, go through a re-tendering process or bring the function back in-house?

Re-tendering provides an opportunity to test the market and establish whether offerings have changed since the contract began. It also means starting again. Organisations should ask themselves whether their objectives have changed as well as analyse their current service provider's performance.

Parties that choose to go their separate ways will enter a phase in the outsourcing life cycle called termination or transition out. The transition-out phase usually begins several months before the contract end date, or transition date, and ends some time after this date – ideally when the buyer is satisfied that the transition was successful.

Look after your assets

There are two key assets in an outsourcing arrangement, and they are carried by the people doing the work: skills and knowledge. Maintaining and caring for these assets means looking after people. A common problem encountered in outsourcing is in-house staff resistance to an altered arrangement. A decision to outsource has a greater adverse effect on staff morale when the news is not communicated to staff. Employees tend to find out about the news anyway. Keeping them well informed is vital since it may lessen some of the employees' concerns and nullify rumours.

Experts in the field, both academics and practitioners, emphasise the importance of communication and involvement. Without these key ingredients, productivity during the changeover period may fall dramatically and key employees may look elsewhere for work. This underlines another important success factor identified by the cases: involving key staff in the outsourcing process allows them to gain a full appreciation of why outsourcing may be the best alternative. Employees may accept the decision to outsource if management explains why the affected staff are being outsourced and the implications of that decision. This may be achieved by involving staff through establishing small project teams that participate in the changeover.

Furthermore, these teams may eventually form the stewardship team, thus ensuring that accountability and management of the relationship are essentially the client's responsibility.

Transfer of personnel is acknowledged as a critical point in the overall success of the arrangement. The change in orientation of the transferred personnel is also considered a success factor. As the employees shift from back office to front office, they must be taught to behave like suppliers. Again, this may be achieved by discussing the positive aspects for personnel, such as the better career development opportunities available at a service provider.

Post-transition, the retention of key knowledge and corporate wisdom is an essential consideration. Collectively, and correctly applied, with focus and concern for maintaining the intellectual capital asset, knowledge work becomes organisational wisdom. The successful organisation nurtures the source of that wisdom – the asset that is the knowledge worker.

That asset literally walks out the door at 5:00 every day. Without proper support, some of those assets may atrophy and some may leave. When the numerous and complicated maintenance requirements of these assets are looked after, then the organisation will own the wisdom generated by them.

Recommendations for service providers

The growth of outsourcing has been dramatic. The ride has been especially dramatic for providers of outsourced services, many of whom have gone through multiple accelerated product life cycles in a very brief time. Given the need for service providers to be hypersensitive to market developments and simultaneously to provide expected service levels, recommendations for service providers run the gamut from macro to micro levels:

- Know your market
- Position for flexibility
- Know your client
- Be proactive
- Keep people
- Get the team right

Know your market

There is a strong tendency, particularly among high-tech companies, to define themselves by their products or offerings rather than the markets they serve (or could serve). The danger in this is the potential to miss opportunities and take an abortive ride on the wrong growth curve by virtue of an inappropriate measure. Market share is not share of "expenditure on organisations just like ours": it should be share of expenditure – by almost anyone – that could potentially be sent our way.

The pace of change in outsourcing and the number of offerings that have developed in short timeframes should emphasise the need for constant monitoring and modification of the parameters of a potential market. The challenges of serving an established client base, however, create a surprising degree of complacency in this regard. Dr. Rashi Glazer defines a "smart" market as one that changes and responds as it interacts with an offering[89]. Outsourcing services are, as highlighted in Chapter Three, ones that are highly interactive and changeable if they are successful. They are operating in a very "smart" market.

"In smart markets, the ability to process information, not the information itself, is the scarce resource."

What vendors of outsourcing services must do without fail is not only collect, but really *use* and *apply* their knowledge of smart markets in which they operate.

Service providers must recognise the full range of potential based on market transformations. Most service providers operate under an assumption that their target market is just large, established companies. This model assumes that control and direction for all business activity, including assignment of tasks and definition of goals and good performance, emanates from the central corporation. In fact, it emanates increasingly from networks and webs of individuals, groups and organisations. The truth is that the centre should be not an organisation, but rather the need for a valued service[90]. From there, the possible providers of a solution come together with the goal of servicing the requirement, not servicing an organisation. Partnerships arise and it should be just as feasible for a current "outsourcer" to be the centre of a web.

Position for flexibility

Rapidly changing markets and multiple learning curves for the industry, for customers and for providers, mean that market agility is essential. Understanding a potential market is not enough. Service providers must be in a position to enter that market most effectively. The tremendous pressure to grow often brings with it a weight that diminishes flexibility. The recommendation to service providers here is to maximise flexibility and the ability to bring precisely customised service to customers by taking a highly modular approach to the design of market offerings. A service offering should be decomposed into its smallest logical subcomponents so that they can be immediately and logically reassembled into an alternate offering that meets customer needs in a customised fashion.

Know your client

Know your client, know the reasons behind the client's decision to outsource, and work towards helping your client succeed and achieve that goal. Don't be surprised by the number of vendors that do this. Do gain advantage by behaving as a "smart" market's vendor does, and make maximum use of all customer knowledge gained.

Along with knowing details behind the client's decision-making about the move to outsource, ensure that you know the client's business and its associated processes. Consider things such as: what is the impact on my client if I fail in my service provsion to them? Know about the client's competitors – try to draw parallels with others where innovative applications have been implemented.

In order to determine the most effective way of providing value to potential and existing customers, suppliers must understand the user's value chain and the essential characteristics of organisations that form links in this chain. Possessing knowledge of the user's business allows a service provider's employees to be seen by the users as 'trusted advisors', rather than 'product-pushers'.

Be proactive

Clients are becoming more sophisticated and more familiar with the detail of measurables that exist in their contracts and are demanding that they receive the standard specified in the contract. Dissatisfaction arises when their vendors are not as familiar as the clients are with standards within the contract. In an increasingly competitive marketplace, suppliers cannot become complacent. Suppliers should take pre-emptive action to ensure that the risks of problems materialising are minimised. Common problems cited by the clients in this research program include: lack of supplier responsiveness; cost escalations due to contract loopholes; inadequate SLAs; use of inexperienced staff; and supplier skills shortages. So make sure you know what your promises are and that you are on track in meeting them.

Keep your people

A service provider's skilled employees are what user organisations are after. Chapter Five presented findings from a multi-company survey analysing what it takes to hold on to employees. People will always be the most important element in a supplier's service proposition.

One of the most common reasons that people leave a job is the receipt of a better offer elsewhere. The most obvious way to circumvent this, especially in highly competitive job categories, is to make the offer first. Offer a raise *before* a competitor comes along with an offer of a higher salary, offer to provide new learning opportunities *before* they are promised at a competitor's site.

Another crucial outsourcing-specific issue related to employee retention is the phenomenon of employee transition. How do you ensure employees are transitioned from customer organisation to service provider organisation successfully? It may help to establish a formal staff mentoring/people management program to help with the smooth transition of employees.

Concerns usually arise from the uncertainty of working for a company different from the one that originally hired the staff member; some employees may feel abandoned, even betrayed. Worse still, lack of formal communication, which details the rationale behind the decision, may translate to the premature departure of the most talented staff. Despite the effectiveness of the HR communication strategy adopted, some employees may leave simply because they do not want their employer to select the organisation that they will be working for.

It is critical to convince employees that the change will result in better career development. This can be achieved by demonstrating that the opportunities for career advancement within a specialist organisation are greater than in a non-specialist company. Staff may also have more opportunities for training within a specialist-focused company. This may help employees keep up to date with changing technology and improve their formal qualifications.

Get the team right

The public face of the service provider organisation is crucial to its success. The sales team should include people from both sales and operations as this ensures congruence between what they say they will deliver and what they can do. This enhances the supplier's ability to "show" the client how it plans on delivering. People want to see in order to believe. This was a common message delivered by the clients in this and previous research.

Once the right team is established, monitor its behaviour. Clients closely analyse the behaviour of the sales team to pick up on intangible aspects or behaviours that they can expect in a relationship. Clients are turned off by "canned presentations". Make a genuine attempt to know the client organisation's business and the industry in which it operates. If possible, use examples from the existing client base to demonstrate this. Many service providers would argue that they would never fall victim to the "canned presentation" routine. But judging from the number of complaints about it, it is more common than most vendors are willing to admit.

Having established a relationship, active management and maintenance is essential. Account management from the vendor includes specifying, contracting and managing the ongoing delivery of services. The case studies emphasise that having the 'right' person in this role is crucial in the perceived success of the relationship. Cultural fit isn't necessarily the most important variable: the relationship is, and the account manager personifies the relationship.

Subsequent promotion of services to the client organisation is best served when adhering to the following relationship principles:

- stay connected with the right parts of the business;
- hold meetings with business owners and General Managers; and
- add value to members higher up in the organisation.

References

[81] *Grover, V., M.J. Cheon, and J.T.C. Teng, "The effects of service quality and partnership on the outsourcing of information systems functions," Journal of Management Information Systems, 1996, 12(4), pp. 89-116.*

[82] *Tapscott, Don, David Ticoll and Alex Lowy, quoted in conversation with Harvard Business School Press's "Power of Ideas @ Work", http://www.hbsp.harvard.edu/ideasatwork, 2000*

[83] *Quinn, "Managing Outsourcing and intellect", op.cit.*

[84] *van der Zee, H.T.M. et al, Successful IT Outsourcing in the Netherlands, unpublished English translation, 1997 (translated from the Dutch Succesvol outsourcen van IT in Nederland, ten Hagen and Stam Uitgevers, Amsterdam, 1997).*

[85] *Lacity, and Willcocks, op.cit.*

[86] *Williamson, op.cit.*

[87] *Law I., Harnessing Outsourcing for Business Advantage, Financial Times Management, London, 1999.*

[88] *Quinn, "Managing Outsourcing and Intellect" op.cit.*

[89] *Glazer,op.cit.*

[90] *Tapscott et al, op. cit.*

Conclusions

This research program has reinforced that the outsourcing market has continued to grow and evolve. Consistent with previous research, we found that the more pervasive and less-high-profile trend of 'selective outsourcing' has become the norm. This is not surprising since it is rare for one supplier to possess the experience and economies of scale to perform all the activities of a particular function most effectively. Instead of corporations trying to be the best at everything, they have accepted they may need to turn to the best. With this new thinking, corporations have also accepted that finding the best in one provider may not be possible.

Although the explicit topic of this book deals with outsourcing, it has implicitly touched on many areas associated with outsourcing and their inter-relationships with the business world. The parameters of business as we have come to know it are transforming. It's all about leveraging skill, knowledge and capabilities to transform an organisation and its relationships with its customers. Outsourcing is simultaneously a symptom and a cause of many of these transformations.

The conventional organisational model is changing irrevocably to include alternative formations. What constitutes being "in" or "out" of an organisation is less and less definitive. The boundary of an organisation is becoming amorphous. The boundary of people's commitments and capabilities are of increasing interest.

Perhaps in the future the corporation as we know it today is going to disintegrate. Internally provided processes and externally provided activities will be intertwined – with a greater reliance on external roles. This change will give companies the flexibility in the marketplace to change direction. Based on the trends identified, the future shape of businesses will involve managing a smaller core operation with an increase in dealings with outside service providers. This will change the expectations surrounding innovation, flexibility and speed.

This situation will remain dynamic for some time. Increasing numbers of viable alternate sources of skill and service provision will continue to drive organisational boundaries and outsourced service provision to places currently unimagined. Reliable, fast, cheap, high-volume communication will increase the reach and possibilities of these alternatives. Virtually any spot on the globe could be a source of skill. Organisations will succeed by merging their operations with the fabric of the Internet. Virtually all knowledge-based organisations will modify their operations to accommodate wide sourcing and increasing levels of collaborative knowledge exchange.

Most outsourcing practitioners are experiencing the phenomena of the early stages of the industry. There is much to be learned from the experiences of those who have gone before, and much to be gained from accepting the inevitability of continued change, innovation and growth. Those organisations that can incorporate the inevitable change into their practices and that welcome it as the harbinger of better things to come are the one that will achieve and sustain success and profit.